BIG GREEN EGG

CERAMIC CHARCOAL

GRILL COOKBOOK

1500 DAYS DELICIOUS, HEALTHY RECIPES THAT ANYONE CAN COOK

JOHN ABBOTT

CONTENTS

INTRODUCTION

What Is A Kamado Grill?

Kamado grills take their name from the term used to describe a traditional Japanese wood or charcoal fueled cooking appliance called a kamado. A traditional kamado was made from clay or other ceramic material to create a large urn or "egg" like vessel, similar to a tandoor, whose round shape and heavy construction allowed unique cooking benefits.

These benefits became clear for our grilling predecessors as they found the ceramic construction provided excellent insulation to keep steady temperatures even at high heat. They found that the superior insulation allows an even cooking process while also being extremely fuel efficient, reducing the amount of charcoal or wood necessary to power the appliance. In addition, the unique shape allowed for several different methods of cooking - whether baking, roasting, smoking, grilling, or any variation, the versatility of these units is unmatched.

In their modern iteration, kamado grills are built of a refractory ceramic material to ensure a high quality durability and heat retention and come in several different sizes and shapes to allow for different configurations. Several accessories and optional components can be purchased for modern kamado grills to alter the way they operate and allow for different cooking methods or distinct grilling advantages.

Heavy Duty Ceramics

As mentioned previously, most kamado grills nowadays feature a heavy duty refractory ceramic that's been industrially designed for maximum durability and insulation. Some gas grills are made from thin metals that can't stay hot when it's cold or windy, that's not the case with kamado grills. The heavy ceramic material absorbs and radiates heat evenly back into the food which is why they make excellent pizza or bread ovens just like a professional brick oven would. What's more, much like the ancient pyramids of Egypt, the ceramic material is designed for the long haul - if properly maintained, your children will inherit your kamado grill.

Fuel Efficient

Another direct benefit of the heavy ceramic construction is the kamado grill's fuel efficiency. Because the thick sides retain heat so well, very little charcoal and oxygen are necessary to continue to fuel the fire - perfect for long, slow cooks or diehard grillers who cook throughout the cold winter. Dampers used to control the intake and exhaust create an airflow that produce a steady flame, when the lid is closed temperatures stay extremely consistent which makes the kamado an excellent choice for smoking ribs, brisket, or pulled pork low and slow and steady temperatures.

Versatile Cooking Methods

Beyond the fuel efficiency, kamado grills have been designed to accommodate a broad spectrum of cooking methods. Accessories like a ceramic heat deflector turn a kamado from a direct grill to an indirect cooker, much like an oven or smoker. Add a firebox divider to create two distinct cooking zones for a true 2-zone setup. With various accessories and setups, a kamado grill can bake, roast, smoke, sear, saute, grill, and much more.

Seeing the Benefits of the Big Green Egg Kamado Grill

1. **True Grilled Food Taste**: Kamado grills like the Big Green Egg use true charcoal or lump charcoal fuel rather than the presoaked charcoal or traditional charcoal and lighter fluid. Cooking in a Kamado style grill provides true smoke and charcoal flavor — not the flavor of the lighter fluid.

2. **Time to Light Fuel Source**: Lump charcoal lights fast and is ready to cook in around 15-30 minutes, depending on the amount of charcoal you are using. Traditional briquettes take 30-45 minutes to be ready for cooking. In addition, a smaller amount of lump charcoal is needed to get the same amount of heat as traditional briquettes.

3. **Temperature Range**: In the Big Green Egg, lump charcoal can reach temperatures of up to 700 degrees. The Kamado grill design allows cooks to maintain steady temperatures for longer periods of time with much less charcoal usage.

4. **Even Heating**: Like traditional gas or charcoal grills, the Big Green Egg has a few hotspots because the fire is seated lower in the grill, thus heating the ceramic walls and distributing it evenly through the dome structure. Heat exits through the top of the dome. The convection-like cooking creates even cooking, quicker cooking, and better cooking.

5. **Ease of Use:** The efficient design allows for fast, simple lighting of the charcoal with a firestarter, not lighter fluid. Kamado grills get up to temperature quickly and it is easy to maintain a steady temperature. Many accessories are available for the Big Green Egg, so cooking is more enjoyable and easy and the result is great tasting food!

6. **Quality of Product:** Kamado grills are designed to last for a very long time. The Big Green Egg has been tested over and over in all sorts of conditions, and with proper care, they will last as long as you want them.

7. **Cleaning:** The efficient design also means that minimal cleaning is required. Because of the efficiency of the charcoal, the ash burns down and cleaning is very simple and is not required as often as with traditional charcoal grills.

8. **Space Needed for Grill:** Kamado grills are relatively compact and can be used in built-in arrangements, as standalone "nests," or with standalone tables designed to house the grill and provide additional workspace for your outdoor grilling and smoking activities.

9. **Multi Purpose:** Kamado grills can be used for direct grilling, indirect grilling, and smoking.

Different Methods on Using Your Big Green Egg Kamado Grill

Using An Electric Starter
1. Open all the air vents all the way
2. Place few pieces of lump charcoal on the bottom of the grill, then place an electric starter on top of it.
3. Wait for about 10-15 minutes before smoke shows up and the charcoal gets burning, then unplug it and remove the electric starter and put it away in a safe place to cool down (remember that it's hot so make sure it's in a safe place).
4. Add some new charcoal, close the lid, adjust the air vents accordingly and wait 15-20 minutes for the grill to reach the right temperature for cooking.

It is not an expensive method, but it is certainly the best one when it comes to getting lump charcoal burning in a kamado.

No chemical additives, doesn't require any tinder, doesn't get your hands messy and is very easy for everyone. It might be a downside that you need to have a source of power nearby which might pose a problem to those staying outside.

Using Charcoal Fire Starters (Lighter Cubes)

1. Obviously, first you have to open all air vents.
2. Place some lump charcoal on the bottom of the grill, then place the recommended amount of charcoal fire starters.
3. Wait a moment for smoke to appear and 10-15 minutes for the charcoal to get hot.
4. Once the charcoal is burning well already, add some new lump charcoal and close the lid of the grill. Leave the air vents open until you reach your desired cooking temperature.

Lighter Cubes are non-toxic and odor-free, the cubes are made of paraffin wax. When burning, they generate a huge flame which allows to get the charcoal burning fast and easily. (The cubes burn for about 10 minutes).

Usually one such cube or alternatively two is enough to get a grill burning, a package containing 24 cubes costs about 4 dollars so I think that it's a pretty cheap and effective solution compared to toxic chemical tinders.

It is also great when combined with the chimney starter method described below.

Using a Charcoal Chimney

1. Remember to open all air vents.
2. Put 2 newspaper sheets on the bottom of the chimney, then fill up the chimney with lump charcoal. If you don't have newspapers, you can put one of the paraffin cubes described above.
3. Next set the newspapers or the cube on fire and wait for 10-15 minutes until all the charcoal gets covered with ash.
4. Pour the hot charcoal into the kamado and fill up the remaining space with even more new charcoal.
5. Close the lid, leave the air vents open and wait for about a dozen minutes until the kamado grill warms up and reaches the right cooking temperature.

What's the advantage of this method ? The charcoal chimney starter makes it possible to get the charcoal burning evenly in a short time without using chemical tinders.

All you need to get charcoal burning in a chimney is some newspaper or lighter cubes (one is enough). Charcoal chimney starter is something that I think every grilling enthusiast should have.

It's an infallible method that allows to get charcoal burning fast and easily without using chemical agents.

Best Way to Clean the Big Green Egg Kamado Grill Grates

Ceramic grill grates are metal grill racks coated with heavy ceramic. It is very durable. When cleaning your ceramic grill, special precautions must be taken so as not to damage the ceramic coating on the grill grates. When you take care of ceramic grill grates and proper maintenance, it will be last for a long time. If you have a ceramic grill, these cleaning tips will help you to keep it looking great for years to come. However, after many uses, ceramic grill grates need good cleaning.

Step 1: Get a soft ceramic grill brush and scouring pad

Ceramic grill grates can chip very quickly if you use a metal or wire-bristle brush. So, avoid using the metal and wire brush on the ceramic grill. Choose a soft bristle brush, such as a sponge brush, nylon brush. The ceramic grill is not at risk of getting damaged when you clean it by nylon brush. You can also use a medium bristle toothbrush and a scouring pad to removing grime from smaller areas.

Step 2: Heat the ceramic grill

The ceramic grill grates will be easier to clean when it is medium hot. Turn on the grill and heat it to burn off any excess food on the ceramic grill grates. Turn off the grill when it becomes red and let it cool for a few minutes so the brush won't melt.

Step 3: Clean the ceramic grill grates properly

Use the soft bristle brush and run it diagonally along the ceramic grill grates. Scrubbed the grill smoothly and lightly, fluid the motion from the bottom to the top of the grates. Run the brush straight over the ceramic grill surface. It will be easier to remove the food derbies and grease on the greats.

Step 4: Repeat Scrubbing

Repeat the scrubbing method until clean the grill grates. Then rains the grill with a wet towel. Let the grill to dry for a few minutes then reuse it.

FISH AND SEAFOOD

Shrimp Stuffed Jalapenos

Servings:2

Cooking Time: 15 Minutes

Ingredients:

- 1 pound of jalapeños
- 4-6 ounces of cream cheese
- 1-2 pounds of shrimp
- 1 pound of bacon
- Seasoning (I like to use Old Bay Blackened Seasoning)

Directions:

1. Preheat the grill to 400°F using direct heat with a cast iron grate installed.

2. Cut the stems off and split the jalapeños in half long ways. Use your knife to cut out the vein through the middle of the jalapeño with all the seeds. If you do not remove the seeds your peppers will be very spicy. After removing the seeds, place the hollowed-out jalapeños into your strainer and rinse them thoroughly.

3. Fill the hollowed-out peppers with cream cheese. Remove the tail from your shrimp, and place a single piece on top of your jalapeno. Wrap your jalapeño with half a slice of bacon and set into a baking dish. Repeat for your entire stock.

4. Once all the jalapeños are wrapped, sprinkle with seasoning. Place the jalapeños on the kamado grill for around 15 minutes, turning them half way through.

5. Remove from the kamado grill and let cool for around 4-5 minutes before serving.

Grilled Shrimp Cocktail With Fire-roasted Cocktail Sauce

Servings:4

Cooking Time: 35 Minutes

Ingredients:

- 1 tablespoon olive oil
- 1⁄2 teaspoon Garlic Salt
- 16 jumbo shrimp (about 1 pound), peeled and deveined 1 cup Fire-Roasted Cocktail Sauce
- 1 tablespoon chopped flat-leaf (Italian) parsley
- 1 lemon, cut into 4 wedges or 8 slices
- 1 cup canned no-salt-added fire-roasted diced tomatoes
- 1 tablespoon horseradish
- 1 tablespoon lime juice
- 1⁄4 teaspoon Chipotle Puree (optional)

Directions:

1. Preheat the grill to 350°F using direct heat with a cast iron grate installed.

2. Combine the oil and garlic salt in a medium bowl. Add the shrimp and toss well.

3. Skewer the shrimp, place the shrimp on the cooking grid and cook for about 3 minutes on each side, or until pink and firm. Remove from the heat.

4. Spoon 1⁄4 cup of cocktail sauce into each of 4 decorative glasses. Top with 4 shrimp per glass. Sprinkle with the parsley and garnish with the lemon wedges or slices.

5. Combine all the ingredients in a blender or food processor and puree until smooth. Transfer the sauce to a jar and chill for at least 30 minutes before using to let the flavors meld. The sauce will keep in the refrigerator for about 1 month.

Lemon Bed Cod

Servings: 6

Cooking Time: 15 Minutes

Ingredients:

- 6 cod filets
- 3 lemons, sliced 1/4 inch thick
- 1 onion, thinly sliced
- Salt & Pepper to taste

Directions:

1. Place lemon slices directly on the grid so they are shingled one on top of another.
2. Place onion slices on top of the lemon.
3. Grilling:
4. Preheat the grill to 400°F using direct heat with a cast iron grate installed.
5. Season both sides of the cod filets with salt and pepper and place them on top of the onion and lemon beds.
6. Close the dome for 12-15 minutes to allow the lemons to steam the fish.
7. Remove the fish on their lemon beds when the fish is opaque. Serve.

Maple-glazed Applewood Smoked Octopus

Servings:4

Cooking Time: 30 Minutes

Ingredients:

- Sushi grade, precooked, octopus tentacles
- 100% Canadian maple syrup

Directions:

1. Defrost the octopus and bring to room temperature.
2. Preheat the grill to 225°F using direct heat with a cast iron grate installed.
3. Place octopus tentacles on the indirect side of grill. Make sure your grid has been cleaned and seasoned with oil as to not tear the octopus while grilling.
4. After a few minutes, start to glaze the octopus tentacles with real 100% Canadian maple syrup. Continue to glaze every five minutes for the next half hour.
5. Remove the octopus from the grill and place onto a plate and open vents fully and open the lid of the kamado grill. Once the coals are red on the direct side, place the octopus on a clean oil-seasoned grill and glaze again.
6. After a minute or less, depending how it's cooking, you will want to flip and glaze the tentacles again. You don't want it so hot that the suction cups fall off, once they start to blacken it's time to flip them one last time with another glaze. Remove the tentacles to a platter and let rest for five minutes.
7. Slice tentacles into ½ inch thick pieces, drizzle one last time with maple syrup and serve. I prefer Kewpie Japanese Mayo, Kentucky Bourbon Barbecue Sauce or Hoison sauce for dipping.

Bacon-wrapped Cod With Roasted Potatoes And Baby Arugula Salad

Servings:8

Cooking Time: 12 Minutes

Ingredients:

- 6-8 slices of thin-cut bacon
- 1 filet of cod
- 10-12 white creamer potatoes, blanched in salt water
- 2 tbsp olive oil
- Salt to taste
- 8 oz baby arugula

- 2 tbsp olive oil
- 1 lemon, zested and squeezed
- Salt to taste

Directions:

1. Preheat the grill to 400°F using direct heat with a cast iron grate installed.

2. Lay the bacon out in strips going away from you, with enough strips to cover the width of the cod. Make sure there are no gaps in the bacon. Lay the cod across the strips of bacon at the end closest to you, and roll the fish one complete turn. Tuck the ends of the bacon tightly under the roll, then continue to roll the cod away from you until you reach the end of the bacon pieces. Place the wrapped cod in a piece of plastic wrap and roll to make sure there is a tight seal. Let rest for 10 minutes.

3. Remove the cod from the plastic wrap. Using toothpicks, secure the ends of the bacon from the opposite side of the fish; you want the toothpick to just barely poke through the bacon on the seam-side, so that the fish lays flat in the skillet. Place the fish seam-side down into the cast iron skillet. While the fish is cooking, toss the potatoes in the olive oil and place directly on the grill around the cast iron skillet. Cook for about 5 minutes.

4. Remove the toothpicks from the fish and flip the fish over. Turn the potatoes to cook evenly. Cook for another 5 minutes.

5. Move the potatoes into the cast iron skillet. Remove the fish from the cast iron skillet and place directly on the grid. Cook for an additional 2 minutes, then remove the potatoes and fish from the kamado grill and let rest.

6. For the salad, mix together the baby arugula, olive oil, salt, lemon zest and lemon juice.

7. Once the fish and potatoes have cooled, cut the cod into 2-inch pieces and then smash the potatoes with palm of a hand. Top with the baby arugula salad and serve!

Red Chili Scallops

Servings:4

Cooking Time: 8 Minutes

Ingredients:

- 3⁄4 cup diced fresh mango
- 1⁄4 cup diced red bell pepper
- 1⁄4 cup diced red onion
- 1⁄4 cup thinly sliced scallions
- 2 tablespoons finely chopped fresh mint
- 1 clove garlic, crushed
- 2 tablespoons freshly squeezed lime juice
- 1 tablespoon extra-virgin olive oil
- 2 teaspoons honey
- 1⁄2 teaspoon kosher salt
- 1⁄4 teaspoon freshly ground black pepper
- 1 pound large sea scallops (12)
- 2 tablespoons Red Chile Rub
- 1 tablespoon cumin seed
- 1 tablespoon coriander seed
- 1 tablespoon red chile flakes
- 1 tablespoon ancho chile powder
- 1 tablespoon kosher salt
- 1 teaspoon sweet paprika
- 1 teaspoon garlic powder

Directions:

1. Set the kamado grill for direct cooking with the Cast Iron Grid.

2. Preheat the grill to 500°F using direct heat with a cast iron grate installed.

3. Using a wooden spoon, combine the mango, bell pepper, red onion, scallions, mint, garlic, lime juice, olive oil, honey, salt, and pepper in a small bowl and stir well. Set aside.

4. Season the scallops generously with the chili rub and place on the Grid. Close the lid of the kamado grill and grill the scallops for about 2 minutes on each side, or until golden and lightly cooked. Transfer the scallops to a platter.

5. To assemble the dish, place 3 scallops on each plate and top with ¼ cup of the salsa. Serve immediately.

6. Toast the cumin seed, coriander seed, and chile flakes in a small skillet on the stovetop for about 5 minutes, or until fragrant. Remove from the heat and allow to cool.

7. Transfer the toasted spices to a spice grinder along with the chile powder, salt, paprika, and garlic powder. Grind for 15 to 20 seconds, until the spices are completely ground. Transfer to an airtight container until ready to use. Makes ½ cup.

Mediterranean Surf And Turf Kabobs

Servings:6
Cooking Time: 20 Minutes

Ingredients:

- 1 lb. boneless leg of lamb (cut into 1 x 1 pieces)
- 1 lb. jumbo shrimp (peeled and deveined)
- 1 red onion (cut into 1 x 1 chunks)
- 1 container baby portobello mushrooms
- 1 container grape tomatoes
- 1 can artichoke hearts
- 1 cup olive oil
- ¼ cup red wine vinegar
- ¼ cup capers (chopped)
- 2 tbsp. fresh oregano (chopped)
- 2 tbsp. fresh rosemary (chopped)
- 2 tbsp. thyme (chopped)
- 1-2 cloves garlic (chopped)
- 1-2 tsp. kosher salt

- ½ tsp. ground black pepper
- ½ tsp. cumin
- ½ tsp. ground coriander

Directions:

1. Preheat the grill to 425°F using direct heat with a cast iron grate installed.

2. You will make 2 different skewers – one will hold the lamb, mushrooms, shrimp and onions. The other will have tomatoes and artichokes. Place the skewers in a pan or dish and pour marinade over them. Toss skewers in marinade and allow marinating for up to 1 hour.

3. Grill the lamb/shrimp skewer for 7-10 minutes or until cooked thoroughly (suggested internal temperature is 135°F). Grill the tomato/artichoke skewer for 3-5 minutes. Take the grilled items off the skewer and serve with either rice or couscous with Tzatziki sauce for a delicious meal!

4. Combine all of the ingredients for the marinade. Set aside.

Thai Shrimp Skewers With Grilled Watermelon Salad

Servings: 4
Cooking Time: 10 Minutes

Ingredients:

- 1-lb U20 shrimp, peeled and deveined
- 4 wooden skewers, soaked in water for 30 minutes
- 1 cup Spicy Thai Marinade
- 1/4 cup olive oil
- 2 Tablespoon rice wine vinegar
- 1 tsp mint leaves, chopped
- 1 tsp fish sauce
- 1 round slice of watermelon, about 1 inch thick

- 1 English cucumber, diced
- 1 Fresno chile, sliced
- 1 shallot, finely diced

Directions:

1. Marinate the shrimp in the Spicy Thai Marinade for 20 minutes in the fridge.

2. In a large bowl, Fresno chile, shallot, vinegar, mint, fish sauce, and olive oil.

3. Grilling:

4. Preheat the grill to 400°F using direct heat with a cast iron grate installed.

5. Thread the shrimp onto the skewers and place on the grid. Close the dome for 3 minutes.

6. Flip the skewers and lower the dome for an additional 3 minutes or until the shrimp are opaque.

7. Brush the watermelon on both sides with olive oil and place on the grid for 30 seconds per side.

8. Dice watermelon and cucumber and stir into dressing.

9. Serve a scoop of the salad with a skewer of shrimp on top.

Bobby Flay's Grilled Lobster Sandwiches

Servings:6
Cooking Time: 28 Minutes

Ingredients:

- 4 (2-pound) live lobsters
- 8 ears of corn
- Kosher salt and freshly ground black pepper
- Canola oil
- 1 serrano chile
- 3 ripe Hass avocados, peeled, pitted, and diced
- 1/4 cup creme fraiche
- 1/2 small red onion, finely diced
- 1/4 cup chopped fresh cilantro leaves
- Juice of 2 limes
- Few dashes of Tabasco sauce
- 6 soft sesame seed buns, split
- Fresh flat-leaf parsley, for garnish

Directions:

1. Bring a large pot of salted water to a boil. Working in batches, add the lobsters and boil for 10 to 12 minutes; they will be about three-quarters done. Drain well and let cool. The lobsters can be parboiled a few hours in advance, covered, and kept refrigerated. Bring to room temperature before grilling.

2. Heat your grill to high for direct grilling.

3. Pull the outer husks down each ear of corn to the base. Strip away the silk from each ear of corn. Fold the husks back into place and tie the ends together with kitchen string. Place the ears of corn in a large bowl of cold water with 1 tablespoon salt for 10 minutes.

4. Remove the corn from the water and shake off the excess. Put the corn on the grill, close the cover, and grill, turning every 5 minutes, for 15 minutes, or until the kernels are almost tender when pierced with a paring knife.

5. Peel back the husks and remove. Brush the corn with oil and season with salt and pepper. Grill the ears until the kernels are lightly golden brown on all sides, about 5 minutes. Use a sharp knife to remove the kernels from the ears.

6. Brush the serrano with oil and grill, turning as needed, until charred all over, 6 to 8 minutes. Remove to a bowl, cover, and let sit for 10 minutes. Peel, seed, and roughly chop.

7. Put the avocados and crème fraîche in a medium bowl and mash slightly with a fork. Add the corn kernels, chile, diced red onion, cilantro,

lime juice, Tabasco, and 2 tablespoons of oil. Season with salt and pepper and gently stir to combine.

8. Split each lobster down the underside with a heavy knife, taking care not to cut through the back shell, so that the lobster is still in one piece but the inside flesh is halved and exposed. Brush the cut sides of the lobsters with oil and season with salt and pepper. Grill the lobsters, cut side down, until lightly charred and heated through, 5 to 7 minutes.

9. Toast the buns, split side down, on the grill until lightly golden brown, about 20 seconds.

10. Remove the lobster meat from the shells and coarsely chop. Fill each bun with lobster, charred corn and avocado, and some parsley leaves.

Florida Lobster Roll

Servings:6
Cooking Time: 28 Minutes

Ingredients:
- 4 tablespoons butter, divided
- Garlic powder
- 3 Florida lobster tails, about 7 ounces each
- ½ cup mayonnaise
- Zest from ½ of a Florida orange
- 1/3 cup finely chopped celery
- Pinch dried tarragon
- 6 hot dog buns, top split if available
- Slices of Florida avocado
- Spinach leaves

Directions:
1. Preheat the grill to 350°F using direct heat with a cast iron grate installed.
2. Split the top of the lobster shells and pull the meat out to rest on top. Cut a few slits in the meat so the lobster will cook evenly (you can have your fish monger do this for you). Place the tails on a perforated cooking grid and season lightly with salt and pepper.

3. Melt two tablespoons of butter and mix in a pinch of garlic powder. Brush the tails liberally with the butter. Place in the kamado grill and cook until the tails are firm to the touch, about 25 minutes; remove and let cool.

4. Remove the platesetter to cook direct at 350°F/177°C. Melt the remaining butter and mix in a pinch of garlic powder. Brush the sides of the rolls and grill them for 2 to 3 minutes on each side until golden brown. Remove the lobster meat from the shells and cut into large dice. Add to the dressing and mix well. Line each bun with a few spinach leaves. Lay a few slices of avocado in the bun and top each with an equal portion of the lobster mix.

5. Mix ingredients together in a large bowl.

Grilled Oysters With Pink Peppercorn Mignonette

Servings:4
Cooking Time: 5 Minutes

Ingredients:
- ½ cup champagne vinegar
- ¼ cup minced shallots
- 1 tablespoon pink peppercorns, crushed
- ¼ cup minced fresh chervil or fresh flat-leaf parsley
- 48 fresh oysters

Directions:
1. Preheat the grill to 500°F using direct heat with a cast iron grate installed.
2. To make the sauce, combine the vinegar, shallots, peppercorns, and chervil in a small bowl and refrigerate.

3. Place the oysters on the grid. Close the lid of the kamado grill and grill for 3 to 4 minutes, until the shells open and release steam. Transfer to a platter. If you have any oysters that do not open, try cooking for a minute or two longer. If they still do not open, discard, as they are not edible. For each oyster, remove the top lid of the shell and separate the oyster from the bottom shell, but do not remove it.

4. Spoon 1 teaspoon of the sauce over each oyster. Serve the oysters immediately in their shells.

Big Game Recipes

Servings:12
Cooking Time: 70 Minutes

Ingredients:
- 1 tablespoon ancho chile powder
- 1 ½ tablespoons onion powder
- 1 ½ tablespoons garlic powder
- 1 tablespoon thyme, dried
- 1 tablespoon black pepper
- ½ teaspoon cinnamon
- 1 tablespoon all-spice
- 1 tablespoon smoked paprika
- ½ teaspoon nutmeg
- 1 each Falconer's Flight hops pellet
- 1 cup sugar
- ½ cup blood orange juice
- ½ cup chicken stock
- 1 pound chicken wings
- 1 cup Dirty Bird Seasoning
- 1 cup clams, chopped
- 3 cups clam juice
- 2 tablespoons butter
- 9 pieces Tater Tots
- 3 pieces bacon
- 1 cup celery, diced small
- 3 cups heavy cream
- 1 cup pearl onions
- Tabasco to taste
- 2 tablespoons all-purpose flour
- 1 bay leaf
- 1 teaspoon thyme, chopped
- Salt to taste
- Pepper to taste

Directions:
1. Combine all ingredients in a bowl until uniformly mixed. Reserve.
2. In saucepot, add all ingredients. Allow to simmer approximately 10 minutes or until the sugar dissolves. Remove the hops pellet. Reserve.
3. Preheat the grill to 350°F using direct heat with a cast iron grate installed.
4. In a bowl, combine Dirty Bird Seasoning and chicken wings until the wings are uniformly coated.
5. Place seasoned chicken wings on the kamado grill and cook for approximately 20, or until an internal temperature of 165°F is achieved. Turn wings to ensure even cooking.
6. Toss cooked chicken wings in the Blood Orange Gastrique and serve hot.
7. Cut bacon into thirds. Wrap around each individual Tater Tot. Place on a perforated baking sheet and bake for 20 minutes or until bacon is crispy. Next preheat cast iron skillet on your grill.
8. Once hot add butter, then saute onions and celery until tender and slightly translucent. Coat cooked vegetables with all-purpose flour then deglaze with clam juice.
9. Next add clams, heavy cream, tabasco, bay leaf, thyme, salt, and pepper. Allow to simmer for 30 minutes.
10. Add bacon wrapped tater tots just before serving. Serve Hot.

Bourbon-glazed Cold Smoked Salmon

Servings:8
Cooking Time: 210 Minutes

Ingredients:

- 2-pound salmon filet, skin on
- 1 tablespoon Makers Mark Bourbon
- 1 orange, zested and sliced into rings
- 1 cup kosher salt
- 2 cups dark brown sugar
- 1 cup Makers Mark Bourbon
- 1/3 cup brown sugar
- ½ cup fig jam
- 1 Tbsp orange juice
- 2 tsp Worcestershire sauce
- ¼ tsp dried mustard
- Pinch of garlic

Directions:

1. Lay the salmon skin-side down on a cutting board. Remove any bones from the flesh and wipe clean of scales. Rinse the salmon with the whiskey and allow to air dry for 10 minutes.

2. In a bowl, combine orange zest, salt and sugar. Line a baking dish with plastic wrap, extending the wrap to allow for wrapping the salmon later. Sprinkle half of the salt mixture on the plastic wrap. Add the salmon and cover with the remaining salt mixture.

3. Lay the orange slices on top of the mixture. Wrap the salmon tightly in the plastic wrap and place in the back of your refrigerator for 48 hours.

4. Once cured, rinse the salmon in cold water. Place the salmon back into the refrigerator, uncovered, for 4 hours.

5. For the glaze, bring bourbon to a boil over medium heat in a saucepan. Add the sugar and whisk, add the remaining ingredients, whisking to blend after each addition. Reduce heat to simmer until sauce is thickened and reduced by half.

6. Preheat the grill to 50°F using direct heat with a cast iron grate installed. Add the salmon to the grid and smoke for 1 hour. Baste the salmon with the bourbon glaze and smoke for an additional 2½ hours.

7. Slice and serve with crackers.

Cioppino (chip-ee-no)

Servings: 6
Cooking Time: 50 Minutes

Ingredients:

- 1 1/2 lbs halibut, or other firm fish, cut into 2 inch chunks
- 1 lb clams, scrubbed
- 1 lb mussels, scrubbed and debearded
- 1 lb shrimp, peeled and deveined
- 4 cloves garlic, minced
- 1 large fennel bulb, thinly sliced
- 1 onion, thinly sliced
- 5 cups chicken or fish stock
- 1 1/2 cups dry white wine
- 1/4 cup tomato paste
- 3 Tablespoons olive oil
- 1 tsp crushed red chile flakes
- 1 (28 ounce) can diced tomatoes

Directions:

1. Preheat the grill to 350°F using direct heat with a cast iron grate installed with the dutch oven on the grid.

2. Heat the oil in the dutch oven and add fennel, onion, and garlic and cook until translucent.

3. Stir in tomato paste and chili flake and cook for 1 minute.

4. Add diced tomatoes with their juice, wine, and stock and cover with the lid.

5. Lower the dome for 30 minutes.

6. Remove the lid of the dutch oven and add the clams and mussels.

7. Replace the lid and lower the dome for 5 minutes.

8. Remove the lid of the dutch oven and add the shrimp and fish and gently stir.

9. Replace the lid and lower the dome for 5 minutes.

10. When the fish is cooked through, the shrimp are pink, and the mussels and clams are open, the stew is done.

11. Serve immediately with crusty sourdough bread.

Shrimp Burgers With Remoulade

Servings: 4
Cooking Time: 10 Minutes

Ingredients:

- 1 lb raw shrimp, peeled & deveined
- 3/4 cups fresh breadcrumbs
- 1/4 cup celery, finely diced
- 1/4 cup green onion, white and light green parts, chopped
- 1/4 cup parsley
- 1 Tablespoon Old Bay Seasoning
- 1 Tablespoon brown mustard
- The juice and zest of 1 lemon
- Olive Oil for brushing
- 1/2 cup mayonnaise
- 2 Tablespoon dill pickle, finely chopped
- 2 tsp prepared horseradish
- 4 hamburger buns
- Shredded lettuce
- Sliced tomato

Directions:

1. In a food processor, combine burger ingredients, minus the breadcrumbs, and process until smooth. Gently fold in breadcrumbs and form into 4 patties. Refrigerate for 20 minutes.

2. Mix remoulade sauce ingredients and refrigerate.

3. Grilling:

4. Preheat the grill to 500°F using direct heat with a cast iron grate installed.

5. Brush both sides of the burgers with olive oil and place directly on the grids. Cover with the dome for 4 minutes.

6. Turn the burgers and cover for another 3 minutes.

7. Close all of the vents and allow the burgers to sit for another 5 minutes or until the burgers reach an internal temperature of 165°F.

8. Place the burgers on bottom buns and top with a dollop of remoulade, sliced tomato, and shredded lettuce.

Savory Pecan Shrimp Scampi Over Spaghetti Squash

Servings: 6
Cooking Time: 50 Minutes

Ingredients:

- 1¼ lbs. large shrimp, peeled and deveined
- 2 tbsp Savory Pecan Seasoning
- 3 tbsp olive oil, divided plus more to coat the pans
- 1 (2-3 pounds) spaghetti squash
- 2 tablespoons unsalted butter
- 3 cloves garlic, minced
- 1 shallot, minced
- ¼ cup dry white wine
- ½ cup fresh basil leaves
- 1 tbsp freshly squeezed lemon juice
- 2 tbsp freshly grated Parmesan

- Kosher salt and freshly ground black pepper, to taste

Directions:

1. Preheat the grill to 375°F using direct heat with a cast iron grate installed.

2. Coat the shrimp with 1 tablespoon extra-virgin olive oil and Savory Pecan Seasoning; then thread them onto the bamboo skewers.

3. Grease the roasting pan with a thin layer of extra virgin olive oil. Cut the squash into 1½ inch rounds; coat with 2 tablespoons extra virgin olive oil and season with salt. Place the squash rounds into the roasting pan, and place on the indirect side of the kamado grill. Roast until tender, about 35-45 minutes. Remove from the kamado grill, and let rest for 10 minutes.

4. Place the Cast Iron Skillet on the indirect side to preheat. Melt butter and a drizzle of olive oil; add garlic and shallots. Cook, stirring occasionally. Add the white wine and let the mixture cook down about 25%.

5. Using a fork, shred the fleshy part of the squash into strands. Add the squash the skillet. Cook, stirring occasionally, until the squash is heated through, about 2-3 minutes. Chiffonade the basil, then add the basil and lemon juice to the skillet; season with salt and pepper to taste.

6. While the skillet mixture is heating, grill the shrimp for 2 minutes on each side on the direct side of the spander. Add the squash "noodles" to a bowl. Serve immediately, topped with shrimp and Parmesan.

Watermelon Pizza

Servings:2
Cooking Time: 12 Minutes

Ingredients:

- 1 Large Watermelon
- 12 Large Shrimp, peeled and deveined
- Sweet & Smoky Seasoning
- 3 TBS olive oil
- 1 cup tomatoes, diced
- 1 Jalapeño, sliced
- 10 sprigs of Cilantro, chopped
- 1 cup of Feta cheese, crumbled
- 4 Bamboo Skewers, soaked
- Salt to taste

Directions:

1. Preheat the grill to 400°F using direct heat with a cast iron grate installed.

2. Skewer the shrimp and season with the olive oil and Sweet & Smoky Seasoning.

3. Cut the Watermelon in a 3-inch diameter. Lightly salt the watermelon.

4. Grill Watermelon 3 minutes on each side and remove from the grill.

5. Grill the shrimp 3 minutes per side and remove from the grill.

6. Build the pizza with the shrimp, feta cheese, jalapeño, tomatoes and cilantro. Grill for another 5 minutes to soften feta and watermelon.

7. Enjoy!

Cardamom Fennel Scallops

Servings:6
Cooking Time: 8 Minutes

Ingredients:

- 1 tsp (2 g) fennel seeds
- 1/2 tsp (1 g) black or yellow mustard seeds
- 1/4 tsp (.5 g) cardamom seeds
- 1 lb. (455 g) large sea scallops (12 to 15)
- 4 medium-sized cloves garlic, finely chopped
- 2 dried red cayenne chilies (like chile de arbol), stems discarded, coarsely chopped (do not remove the seeds)
- 1 tsp (6 g) coarse kosher or sea salt

- 2 tbsp (30 ml) canola oil
- 1/2 cup (125 ml) unsweetened coconut milk
- 1 tbsp (2 g) finely chopped fresh cilantro leaves and tender stems

Directions:

1. Place the fennel, mustard and cardamom seeds in a spice grinder (or a coffee grinder) and grind them to the consistency of finely ground black pepper (and be sure to take a good sniff as you open the lid…just be prepared for a burst of flavor!) Transfer the spice blend to a medium-size bowl.

2. Add the scallops, garlic, chilies and salt to the bowl with the spice blend and stir to mix, making sure you coat the scallops well. Refrigerate the scallops, covered, until you are ready to cook them; keep in mind that since there is nothing acidic in this mix, you can easily marinate the scallops overnight.

3. Preheat the grill to 400°F using direct heat with a cast iron grate installed.

4. When you are ready to cook the scallops, heat the oil in our combination Stir-Fry and Paella Grill Pan until the oil appears to shimmer. Add the scallops, rub and all, to the skillet, arranging them in a single layer. Sear the scallops until they are light reddish brown, 2 to 3 minutes per side.

5. Pour the coconut milk into the pan; the coconut milk will immediately start to bubble in the hot pan. Crape the bottom of the pan to release al the browned bits, effectively deglazing the pan to create a depth of the scallops simmer, without stirring, until they are firm to the touch, about 2 minutes. Transfer the scallops to a serving platter.

6. Let the sauce continue to simmer, stirring occasionally, until thickened, about 2 minutes.

Pour the pan sauce over the scallops. Serve the scallops warm, sprinkled with the cilantro. Enjoy!

Grilled Rockefeller Oysters

Servings:12
Cooking Time: 5 Minutes

Ingredients:
- 12 shucked oysters
- 1/4 cup butter
- 1/2 cup red onions (chopped)
- 4 cloves garlic
- 1/2 cup Pinot Grigio
- 21/2 cups spinach (roughly chopped)
- 2 tbsp heavy cream
- 2 tbsp clam juice
- 1/2 cup mozzarella
- 2 tbsp crunchy bacon (chopped finely)

Directions:

1. Preheat the grill to 375°F using direct heat with a cast iron grate installed.

2. In a Stir-Fry and Paella Pan or other grill-safe pan, sauté onions in 2 tbsp butter on medium high until slightly translucent. Add Pinot Grigio and simmer for 2 minutes. Add the rest of the butter and garlic and cook for 1 minute. Add spinach and cook until spinach is wilted, and then add the heavy cream and clam juice and cook for a few more seconds.

3. Top oysters with spinach mixture and mozzarella and place on a Perforated Cooking Grid or directly on the cooking grid for about 5 minutes or until the cheese bubbles. Sprinkle with bacon and enjoy!

Foil Packet Fish Filets

Servings: 4
Cooking Time: 15 Minutes

Ingredients:

- 4 (4 oz each) white fish filets
- 1/2 cup white wine
- 4 Tablespoons butter
- 4 pieces heavy duty foil
- 4 sprigs fresh thyme
- 4 green onions, cut in thirds
- 1 zucchini, julienned
- 1 large carrot, julienned
- 1 clove garlic, minced

Directions:

1. On the bottom of each foil sheet, place zucchini, carrot and onion to create a bed.
2. Place one fish filet on each bed of vegetables and top with garlic, thyme, 1 Tbs of butter, salt and pepper to taste.
3. Gather two sides of the foil together and fold down so the foil is almost touching the food.
4. Roll one side of the foil then pour in 2 Tablespoon of white wine. Close the remaining side. Repeat
5. Grilling:
6. Preheat the grill to 375°F using direct heat with a cast iron grate installed.
7. Place the foil packets on the grid and close the dome for 12-15 minutes or until the fish is cooked through.

Oysters On The Half Shell

Servings: 4
Cooking Time: 9 Minutes

Ingredients:

- 16 whole oysters
- 1/2 cup butter, softened
- 2 Tablespoons fresh parsley
- 2 cloves garlic, minced
- The zest of 1 lemon

Directions:

1. In a small bowl, combine butter, parsley, garlic, and lemon zest. Set aside
2. Grilling:
3. Preheat the grill to 425°F using direct heat with a cast iron grate installed.
4. Place the cleaned oysters, cup side down, directly on the grids and close the dome for 7-9 minutes or until the oysters open up.
5. Remove the top shells and spoon in equal portions of the compound butter. Close the dome for 1 minute more until the butter melts and serve.

Surf Perch

Servings:3
Cooking Time: 10 Minutes

Ingredients:

- 3 Surf Perch, 1-3 pounds each
- Olive oil
- Sea salt and ground black pepper to taste
- Hickory smoking chunks

Directions:

1. Scale and gut the fish, leaving the heads on. Lay them on their side on tinfoil. Pour olive oil over each fish. Sprinkle heavily with ground sea salt and ground pepper.
2. Preheat the grill to 400°F using direct heat with a cast iron grate installed. You want a lot of smoke because the fish will only be cooking for a short amount of time, and they still have their skin on so the smoke will need to penetrate it.
3. Place the fish (still on the tin foil) on the cooking grid and cook until the fish are brown and smoky.
4. The meat will fall off the bones and have a wonderfully smoky flavor. Bon Appetite!

Country Ham, Shrimp & Grits Kabobs

Servings:8
Cooking Time: 67 Minutes

Ingredients:

- 1 cup grits
- 1 cup shredded cheddar
- ¼ cup Oliver Farms Pecan Oil or Butter
- 1 cup country ham, fine dice
- ½ cup diced scallions
- ½ cup red pepper, fine dice
- ½ cup yellow pepper, fine dice
- 1 cup heavy cream
- 4 cups water
- 2 tsp salt
- ½ tsp black pepper
- ½ tsp dried thyme
- 1 pound 26-30 count shrimp, peeled and deveined, tail on
- ¼ cup olive oil
- 1 Tbsp Dijon mustard
- 1 tsp minced garlic
- 2 Tbsp fresh lemon juice
- Salt and pepper
- 1 red pepper, seeded, membrane removed, cut in 1" squares
- 1 yellow pepper, seeded, membrane removed, cut in 1" squares
- 1 red onion, peeled, cut in 1" squares, separate layers

Directions:

1. Cook diced ham in butter or oil until almost crisp. Add diced peppers and scallions. Cook until soft. Add cream, water and spices. Bring to a boil, gradually stir in grits. Bring back to a boil, then lower to simmer. Continue cooking for 45-60 minutes, adding a little more liquid if needed; they need to be thick. Remove from heat and stir in cheese until melted. Pour into greased 9" x 13" pan. Chill overnight.

2. Combine olive oil, Dijon, garlic, lemon juice, salt and pepper in a bowl. Add shrimp to mixture and marinate about 30 minutes

3. Cut grits into 1 square. Broil in oven on both sides until golden. Thread wooden skewers with 1 grits cube then pierce one piece each of red pepper, yellow pepper and red onion. Chill until ready to use.

4. Preheat the grill to 350°F using direct heat with a cast iron grate installed. Place skewers on the cooking grid; close dome and cook 5-7 minutes or until shrimp are opaque. Use spatula to carefully lift from underneath.

Grilled Oysters With Garlic Butter

Servings:4
Cooking Time: 5 Minutes

Ingredients:

- A dozen fresh oysters (the fresher, closer-to-home you can get the better!)
- 6 Tbsp – a little more than half a package – slow-cultured, Roasted Garlic Basil & Parsley Banner Butter
- 1 lemon, cut into slices or wedges
- 3 Tbsp fresh chives, roughly chopped

Directions:

1. Preheat the grill to 425°F using direct heat with a cast iron grate installed.

2. Take your Roasted Garlic Basil & Parsley Banner Butter out of the fridge and set aside in a small bowl.

3. Carefully shuck the oysters with a small knife (an oyster knife with a rounded tip and a work

glove on the hand grasping the oyster is a good choice for novice shuckers). Remove the top, flat shell and discard. Place the rounded (bowl side of the shell) side with the oyster on a Perforated Cooking Grid.

4. Place the Perforated Grid in the kamado grill and then add a half tablespoon of softened Roasted Garlic butter to each oyster.

5. Close the lid and kamado grill for 4 or 5 minutes until the oysters are bubbling (not rubbery). The butter should be completely melted and beginning to caramelize on the shell when done.

6. Remove from the kamado grill and move the oysters to a serving plate with the lemons. Squeeze a few wedges/slices onto the oysters and then scatter the chives across the plate.

Grilled Shrimp And Taylor Farms Tangerine Crunch Wraps

Servings:2
Cooking Time: 6 Minutes

Ingredients:
- 1 lb. large shrimp, peeled and deveined
- Savory Pecan Seasoning
- 4-6 sundried tomato or spinach wraps
- 1 Taylor Farms Tangerine Crunch Chopped Kit
- bamboo skewers, soaked
- Feta cheese, optional

Directions:
1. Preheat the grill to 400°F using direct heat with a cast iron grate installed.

2. Season the shrimp on both sides with the Savory Pecan Seasoning. Skewer the shrimp with the soaked skewers.

3. Place the shrimp on the kamado grill and cook for 3 minutes per side or until the shrimp are pink and firm. Remove from the grill, cool and remove from the skewers.

4. Heat a plancha on the grill, griddle-side up.

5. Mix together the Taylor Farms Tangerine Crunch Chopped Kit. Fill the wrap with the salad, top with shrimp and feta cheese. Roll the wrap to enclose the salad. Heat the wrap on the plancha until you have your desired grill marks. Remove from the kamado grill and serve.

Grill-roasted Arctic Char

Servings:4
Cooking Time: 27 Minutes

Ingredients:
- Butcher twine
- 2 leeks, trimmed, leaves separated and washed (16 leaves needed) 1 pear
- 1 sweet onion, thinly sliced into rings
- 1/2 cup (125 mL) fresh sage leaves
- Pinch of ground cinnamon
- Pinch of cayenne pepper
- Sea salt and freshly ground black pepper to taste
- 1 orange, halved
- 1 tbsp (15 mL) melted butter
- 2 arctic char fillets (approx. 8 oz/225 g each), skin on 4 to 5 slices bacon

Directions:
1. In a pot of boiling water, blanch the leek leaves for 1 minute or until tender and bright. Cool in ice water. Drain on paper towels.

2. Using a sharp knife, slice the pear into thin slices, cutting from the top of the pear to the bottom so that you get a cross-section of pear. Remove seeds. Place in a bowl. Add sliced onions and sage leaves and season with a little pinch of

cinnamon, cayenne pepper, sea salt and black pepper. Squeeze the orange halves over top. Add melted butter and mix well. Set aside.

3. Using a sheet of plastic wrap a little longer than each of the fish fillets, lay 6 to 8 pieces of blanched leek onto the plastic, slightly overlapping. Place 1 fillet of arctic char, skin side down, crosswise across the middle of the leeks. Season the char fillet with a little salt and black pepper. Spread the stuffing mixture over the entire surface of the char.

4. Season the second fillet of arctic char with a little salt and black pepper. Lay fillet skin side up on the onion-pear stuffing. Starting on the edge closest to you, roll the leeks around the fish to make a tight leek wrap.

5. Next run your fingers along the top side of the bacon, pressing firmly to stretch the slice of bacon by about 25%. Wrap the bacon around the leek in three separate bands, leaving a swatch of leek in between. Cut 3 to 5 strips of butcher twine, each about 10 to 12 inches (25 to 30 cm) in length. Wrap one string around one strip of bacon and tie tightly around the fish bundle. Repeat with other strips of bacon and add a couple more if necessary. You don't want this bundle to fall apart. Cover and refrigerate to rest for 1 hour.

6. Preheat the grill to 400°F using direct heat with a cast iron grate installed.

7. Place the fish bundle onto the kamado grill directly over the heat. Grill for 10–12 minutes with the dome open, watching for flare-ups, until the bacon starts to crisp and you can see some juices come

8. from the fish. Using spatula, carefully turn fish over. Reduce grill heat and close dome. Continue to grill for another 10–15 minutes, until the bacon is crisp and the fish is just cooked through; ensure the stuffing is hot. Use a small metal skewer to test for doneness. Poke it in, and if it comes out hot, it's ready to go!

9. Remove from kamado grill. Remove butcher twine. Slice stuffed char into 2-inch (5 cm) thick slices. Serve immediately.

Shrimp And Grits Kabobs

Servings:4
Cooking Time: 67 Minutes

Ingredients:

- ¼ cup Pecan oil or butter
- 1 cup country ham finely diced
- ½ cup diced scallions
- ½ cup red pepper finely diced
- ½ cup yellow pepper finely diced
- 1 cup heavy cream
- 4 cups water
- 2 teaspoons salt
- ½ teaspoons black pepper
- ½ teaspoon dried thyme
- 1 cup grits
- 1 cup cheddar cheese, shredded
- 1 pound shrimp, 26-30 count, pealed and deveined, tail on
- ¼ cup olive oil
- 1 Tablespoon Dijon mustard
- 1 teaspoon minced garlic
- 2 Tablespoons fresh lemon juice
- salt and pepper
- 1 red pepper, seeded and membrane removed, cut into 1 inch squares
- 1 yellow pepper, seeded and membrane removed, cut into 1 inch squares
- 1 red onion, peeled, cut in 1 inch squares, separate layers

Directions:

1. Cooked diced ham in butter or oil until almost crisp. Add diced peppers and scallions. Cook until soft. Add cream, water and spices. Bring to a boil, gradually stir in grits. Bring to a boil, them lower to simmer. Continue cooking for 45-60 minutes adding a little more liquid if needed; they need to be thick. Remove from heat and stir in cheese until melted. Pour into greased Rectangular Drip Pan. Chill over night.

2. Combine olive oil, Dijon mustard, garlic, lemon juice, salt and pepper in a bowl. Add shrimp to mixture and marinate about 30 minutes.

3. Cut grits into 1 inch squares. Broil in oven on both sides until golden. Thread Flexible Skewers with 1 grits cube then pierce on one piece each of shrimp, red pepper, yellow pepper, and red onion. Chill until ready to use.

4. Preheat the grill to 350°F using direct heat with a cast iron grate installed. Place skewers on plate setter; close dome and cook 5-7 minutes or until shrimp are opaque.

5. Use spatula to carefully lift from underneath.

Maryland Crab Cakes

Servings: 4

Cooking Time: 15 Minutes

Ingredients:

- 1⁄2 cup crushed saltine crackers
- 1 tsp mustard
- 1⁄2 tbsp Old Bay Seasoning
- 1⁄4 tsp kosher salt
- 1 large egg, beaten
- 2 tbsp mayonnaise
- 1⁄2 tsp Worcestershire sauce
- 1lb (450g) fresh lump crabmeat, such as blue crab
- 1 tbsp chopped fresh flat-leaf parsley
- 1 tbsp canola oil
- 1 tbsp unsalted butter, melted
- for the remoulade
- 1⁄2 cup mayonnaise
- 1 tbsp prepared horseradish
- 1 tbsp sriracha
- 1 tbsp capers
- 1 tbsp apple cider vinegar
- 1 tbsp lemon juice
- 2 tsp Dijon mustard
- 1 shallot, coarsely chopped

Directions:

1. To make the remoulade, in a food processor, combine mayonnaise, horseradish, sriracha, capers, vinegar, lemon juice, mustard, and shallot until smooth. Pour mixture into a small bowl, cover with plastic wrap, and refrigerate until ready to serve.

2. In a small bowl, combine crackers, mustard, Old Bay Seasoning, and salt. In a large bowl, combine egg, mayonnaise, and Worcestershire sauce. Fold in the cracker mixture, and add crabmeat and parsley. Shape the mixture into small cakes, ensuring not to break up the crabmeat, and refrigerate for 1 hour. (This will prevent the cakes from falling apart while cooking.)

3. Preheat the grill to 400°F (204°C) using indirect heat with the heat deflector and a cast iron skillet installed. Place oil and butter in the skillet, add the crab cakes to the skillet, close the lid, and cook until golden brown and the internal temperature reaches 140°F (60°C), about 15 minutes, flipping halfway through.

4. Remove the crab cakes from the grill. Serve immediately or keep warm in a 200°F (93°C) oven, and top with the remoulade.

Spice-crusted Salmon With Rosé-glazed Vegetables

Servings:4

Cooking Time: 9minutes

Ingredients:

- 2 filets of salmon, skin off
- Classic Steakhouse Seasoning
- Hummus
- Kalamata olives
- Marinated artichokes
- Peppadew peppers, can substitute with roasted red bell peppers
- Roasted garlic
- ½ cup of rosé wine

Directions:

1. Preheat the grill to 400°F using direct heat with a cast iron grate installed, with a cast iron grate, flat sideup, and a cast iron skillet.

2. Liberally add the Classic Steakhouse Seasoning to the salmon and pat to adhere. Oil the cast iron grate, pat the salmon to get any access moisture off and place on the cast iron grate.

3. Remove from the grill. Serve the salmon over the hummus with the vegetables.

4. Add the roasted garlic and peppadew peppers to the cast iron skillet, cook for about 3-4 minutes.

5. Add the artichokes, olives and wine to the cast iron skillet. Flip the salmon and continue to cook for another 5 minutes

Grilled Shrimp Salad

Servings:4

Cooking Time: 5 Minutes

Ingredients:

- 1 ¼ pounds large fresh shrimp, peeled and deveined
- 1 tablespoon plus 3 tablespoons olive oil
- 3 tablespoons fresh orange juice
- 1 teaspoon grated orange zest
- 3 tablespoons sherry vinegar
- 3 tablespoons honey
- 3 tablespoons chopped fresh mint
- ½ teaspoon salt
- ¼ teaspoon freshly ground black pepper
- 6 cups mesclun mix, baby arugula, torn frisee (French curly endive) or other greens
- 2 large vine-ripened tomatoes, cored and diced
- 1 cup garlic-flavored croutons
- 4 ounces Cabot Monterey Jack or Cabot Mild Cheddar, grated (about 1 cup)

Directions:

1. Preheat the grill to 500°F using direct heat with a cast iron grate installed.

2. In medium bowl, toss shrimp with 1 tablespoon oil. Thread shrimp on flexible skewers. Place on kamado grill and cook until pink, about 2 minutes per side. Remove from heat; slide shrimp off skewers onto plate.

3. In small bowl, whisk together orange juice and zest, vinegar, remaining 3 tablespoons oil, honey, mint, salt and pepper.

4. Divide greens among 4 plates. Top with tomatoes, croutons and shrimp. Drizzle each with one fourth of dressing. Top with cheese.

Miso Poached Sea Bass

Servings: 4

Cooking Time: 55 Minutes

Ingredients:

- 4 large eggs
- 3 tbsp white miso paste

- 4 sea bass fillets, about 6oz (170g) each, skinned and deboned
- 3 medium red-skinned potatoes
- 12 fresh green beans
- 1 red onion
- 1 medium head of butter lettuce
- 2 large beefsteak tomatoes, sliced
- 16 Kalamata olives, pitted
- 4 tbsp capers
- 2 tbsp chopped fresh flat-leaf parsley
- for the dressing
- 4 garlic cloves, crushed
- 2 tsp Dijon mustard
- 6 tbsp extra virgin olive oil
- 2 tbsp soy sauce
- 2 tbsp white miso
- 3 tbsp rice vinegar
- kosher salt and freshly ground black pepper
- to smoke
- grapevine or apple wood chunks

Directions:

1. Place eggs in a medium saucepan and cover with cold water. Cover the pot with a lid and bring to a boil on the stovetop over high heat. Once boiling, remove the pot from the heat, keep it covered, and let sit for 20 minutes. Drain the water, and set eggs aside to cool. Once cool, peel, halve, and refrigerate until ready to use.

2. To make the dressing, in a small bowl, whisk together garlic, Dijon mustard, oil, soy sauce, miso, and rice vinegar. Season with salt and pepper to taste, and set aside.

3. Preheat the grill to 425°F (218°C) using direct heat with a cast iron grate installed. Add enough water in the dutch oven to cover bass. (Don't add bass to the water yet.) Place the dutch oven on the grate, leave the lid off the dutch oven, and close the grill lid.

4. Once the water starts to simmer, place the wood chunks on the coals. Add miso paste, stirring to dissolve, and then add fish fillets. Leave the lid off the dutch oven, close the grill lid, and cook until cooked through, about 10 minutes per inch of thickness. Remove from the water and set aside.

5. Place potatoes, green beans, and onion on the grate around the dutch oven. Close the lid and grill until charred, about 7 to 10 minutes. Remove the vegetables from the grill, and chop potatoes and onion. Place the vegetables in a medium bowl, add the dressing, and stir to coat.

6. Line a serving platter with the large outer lettuce leaves. Chop the remainder and arrange on the platter. Place tomato slices on one end of the platter, followed by the grilled vegetables. (Don't throw out the dressing from the bowl.) Place fish in the center of the platter. Garnish with sliced hard-boiled eggs, olives, and capers. Sprinkle parsley over top and drizzle the remaining dressing before serving.

Grilled Whole Trout

Servings: 2
Cooking Time: 20 Minutes

Ingredients:

- 2 whole trout (about 1 lb each), cleaned and gutted
- 2 Tablespoons olive oil
- 1/2 tsp salt
- 1/4 tsp pepper
- 4 cloves garlic, smashed
- 1/2 sliced lemon
- 1/2 bunch fresh parsley

Directions:

1. Brush the inside of the cavity and outside of the fish with olive oil and season with salt and pepper.

2. Stuff lemon, garlic, and parsley inside the cavity of each fish.

3. Grilling:

4. Preheat the grill to 400°F using direct heat with a cast iron grate installed.

5. Place the fish directly on the grid and close the dome for 10 minutes.

6. Gently flip the fish and close the dome for an additional 5-10 minutes or until the fish is cooked through.

Cajun Shrimp Burgers

Servings:4

Cooking Time: 12 Minutes

Ingredients:

- 1 – 1 1/2 pounds raw shrimp, peeled and deveined
- 4 tablespoons olive oil or coconut oil, divided
- 1 small shallot, finely minced (about 2-3 tablespoons)
- 1 small clove garlic, finely minced
- 1/4 cup red or yellow pepper, finely minced
- 1 teaspoon sea salt
- 1/2 teaspoon freshly ground pepper
- 1 teaspoon chili powder
- 1 teaspoon paprika
- 1 teaspoon cayenne pepper
- 1 teaspoon Dijon mustard
- 1 teaspoon fresh lemon juice
- 1 tablespoon of worcestershire sauce
- 1 large egg, beaten

- 1 green onion, chopped
- 3/4 cup of Coconut Cream (place a can in the refrigerator overnight and scoop the top for the cream and save the rest for your smoothie) or Paleo Mayonnaise
- 1 tablespoon of dijon mustard
- 1 tablespoons of all natural ketchup
- 1 teaspoon of worcestershire sauce
- 1 teaspoon horseradish
- 1 teaspoon of Paprika
- 1 teaspoon fresh lemon juice
- 1/2 teaspoon Cayenne
- 1/2 teaspoon chili powder
- 1/2 teaspoon of Salt

Directions:

1. Preheat the grill to 425°F using direct heat with a cast iron grate installed.

2. Add shrimp to your food processor and pulse until mixture is in small pieces. Remove and place in a mixing bowl.

3. In a small sauté pan, heat 1 tablespoon oil over medium heat. Add shallot, garlic and peppers; cook for about 4 minutes, until softened. Season with salt and pepper. Remove from heat and let cool. Add the remaining ingredients then cooled pepper mixture to the shrimp bowl and combine well. Mold to your desired burger size and set on a plate then cover and refrigerate for 30 minutes.

4. Meanwhile in a small bowl, combine mayonnaise ingredients and set aside.

5. Cook burgers on the Cast Iron Grid for 3-4 minutes per side, until golden brown and cooked through.

BURGERS

Breakfast Burger

Servings: 4

Cooking Time: 13 Minutes

Ingredients:

- 1 1/2 lb ground beef
- 1/2 lb ground pork breakfast sausage
- 2 Tablespoon butter
- 8 strips bacon
- 4 slices sharp cheddar cheese
- 4 Brioche buns
- 4 eggs
- 4 thick slices tomato

Directions:

1. In a medium bowl, mix ground beef and sausage until just combined.

2. Form into 4 patties and refrigerate while the grill heats.

3. Melt butter in a large skillet and fry the eggs for 2 minutes on each side.

4. Grilling:

5. Preheat the grill to 400°F using direct heat with a cast iron grate installed.

6. Place bacon on a small cookie sheet and place on the grid in the grill. Cook until crispy.

7. Place the patties on the grid and close the dome for 3 minutes.

8. Flip the burgers and replace the dome for an additional 3 minutes.

9. Close all of the vents and allow the burgers to sit for an additional 5 minutes. The internal temperature of the burger should be 150°F.

10. Place cheese on top of the burgers and cover for 1 more minute.

11. Assemble the burgers by placing a burger on the bottom bun, topping with bacon, tomato, and a fried egg.

Classic American Burger

Servings: 4

Cooking Time: 12 Minutes

Ingredients:

- 2 lbs ground beef
- 1/2 tsp salt
- 1/4 tsp pepper
- 4 slices American cheese
- 4 hamburger buns
- Green Leaf Lettuce
- Sliced Tomato
- Ketchup
- Mustard
- Sliced Pickle

Directions:

1. Form ground beef into four patties and season both sides with salt and pepper.

2. Grilling:

3. Preheat the grill to 500°F using direct heat with a cast iron grate installed.

4. Place burgers on the grid and close the dome for 3 minutes.

5. Flip burgers and close the dome for 2 more minutes.

6. Close all of the vents and allow the burgers to sit for 5 minutes.

7. Top each burger with a slice of cheese and close the dome for 1 more minute.

8. Build burgers with lettuce, tomato, pickle, mustard, and ketchup.

Oahu Burger

Servings: 4

Cooking Time: 12 Minutes

Ingredients:

- 2 lbs ground beef
- 1/4 cup thickened Teriyaki Marinade
- 1/4 cup mayonnaise
- 1/2 tsp sambal or sriracha
- 4 slices fresh pineapple, cored
- 4 slices tomato
- 4 slices butter lettuce
- 4 Hawaiian hamburger buns

Directions:

1. Form ground beef into four patties and season both sides with salt and pepper.

2. In a small bowl, mix mayonnaise with hot chile sauce and spread on buns.

3. Top each bun with a burger, slice of pineapple, lettuce and tomato.

4. Grilling:

5. Preheat the grill to 500°F using direct heat with a cast iron grate installed.

6. Place burgers on the grid and close the dome for 3 minutes.

7. Flip burgers, baste with Teriyaki Marinade, and place the pineapple slices on the grid. Close the dome for 2 more minutes.

8. Flip the burgers again and baste with remaining Teriyaki Marinade. Close the dome.

9. Close all of the vents and allow the burgers to sit for 5 minutes.

Quesadilla Burger

Servings: 4

Cooking Time: 12 Minutes

Ingredients:

- 2 lbs ground beef
- 2 Tablespoons Adobo Rub
- 1 cup shredded cheddar cheese
- 4 large flour tortillas
- Sour Cream
- Guacamole
- Salsa

Directions:

1. Form ground beef into four patties and season both sides with Adobo Rub.

2. Serve each burger with sour cream, guacamole, and salsa.

3. Grilling:

4. Preheat the grill to 500°F using direct heat with a cast iron grate installed.

5. Place burgers on the grid and close the dome for 3 minutes.

6. Flip burgers and close the dome for 2 more minutes.

7. Close all of the vents and allow the burgers to sit for 5 minutes.

8. Remove burgers and place flour tortillas on the grid.

9. Top each tortilla with shredded cheese and close the dome for 1 minute until the cheese melts.

10. Place a hamburger in the center of each tortilla and begin folding the tortilla around the burger like an envelope.

The Crowned Jewels Burger

Servings: 4

Cooking Time: 12 Minutes

Ingredients:

- 2 lbs ground beef
- 1/2 tsp salt
- 1/4 tsp pepper
- 1 lb thinly sliced pastrami
- 1 cup shredded Romaine lettuce

- 1/4 cup mayonnaise
- 2 Tablespoons ketchup
- 1/8 tsp onion powder
- 4 slices Sharp Cheddar cheese
- 4 hamburger buns
- 1 tomato, sliced

Directions:

1. Form ground beef into four patties and season both sides with salt and pepper.
2. Meanwhile, mix together mayonnaise, ketchup, and onion powder. Smear on each bun.
3. Place each pastrami and cheese covered burger on the prepared buns and top with shredded lettuce and tomato.
4. Grilling:
5. Preheat the grill to 500°F using direct heat with a cast iron grate installed.
6. Place burgers on the grid and close the dome for 3 minutes.
7. Flip burgers and close the dome for 2 more minutes.
8. Close all of the vents and allow the burgers to sit for 5 minutes.
9. Top each burger with 1/4 of the pastrami and a slice of cheese and close the dome for 1 more minute.

"the Masterpiece"

Servings: 4
Cooking Time: 12 Minutes

Ingredients:

- 2 lbs ground beef
- 6 ounces sliced mushrooms
- 4 Tablespoons shredded smoked Gouda
- 2 Tablespoons butter
- 2 Tablespoons olive oil
- 2 Tablespoons Dijon mustard
- 1/2 tsp salt

- 1/4 tsp pepper
- 8 slices bacon, cooked and crumbled
- 4 slices Swiss cheese
- 4 brioche buns
- 1 small onion, sliced

Directions:

1. Heat a skillet over medium heat and add 1 Tablespoon butter and 1 Tablespoon olive oil.
2. Place mushrooms in the pan and DO NOT MOVE THEM. Saute for 5-7 minutes or until the mushrooms are browned. Remove from the pan and set aside.
3. In the same skillet, heat remaining butter and olive oil and add onions. Saute over medium heat until they become translucent and begin to brown, about 10 minutes. Remove from the heat and set aside to cool.
4. Mix onion, mushrooms, and crumbled bacon.
5. Grilling:
6. Preheat the grill to 425°F using direct heat with a cast iron grate installed.
7. Form ground beef into eight patties and season both sides with salt and pepper.
8. Place a generous spoonful of the mushroom and onion mixture in the center of four patties and top with smoked Gouda.
9. Top with additional patty and press sides to seal the mixture inside.
10. Place burgers on the grid and close the dome for 5 minutes.
11. Flip burgers and close the dome for 3 more minutes.
12. Close all of the vents and allow the burgers to sit for 5 minutes.
13. Top each burger with a slice of Swiss cheese and close the dome for 1 more minute.
14. Spread buns with mustard, top with burgers and bun tops.

POULTRY

The Perfect Roasted Turkey

Servings:4

Cooking Time: 12 Minutes

Ingredients:

- 1 turkey, cleaned thoroughly
- poultry seasoning
- 1 whole onion cut in half
- 1 stalk celery
- 2 cups chicken broth, wine or water

Directions:

1. Preheat the grill to 325°F using direct heat with a cast iron grate installed. Use a handful of pecan chips for a light, smoky flavor and to provide a deep brown color to the turkey.

2. Spread the seasoning generously over the outside of the bird. Load the bird onto a Vertical Poultry Roaster or Rib and Roasting Rack, then place into a drip pan. Add the onion and celery to the drip pan. Fill the pan with chicken broth, wine, or water.

3. Cook for 12 minutes per pound until the turkey has reached a safe minimum internal temperature of 165°F throughout the product. Reserve the drippings from the drip pan to make gravy.

Wickles Brine Blasted Chicken

Servings:8

Cooking Time: 90 Minutes

Ingredients:

- 1 whole chicken (4-5 lb)
- 1 Wickles Jar w/ Brine (pickles eaten or reserved)
- 4 tbsp olive oil
- Rub of your choice
- 1 head garlic (sliced in half lengthwise)
- 3-4 fresh dill sprigs

Directions:

1. Preheat the grill to 325°F using direct heat with a cast iron grate installed.

2. Rise chicken and pat dry. Coat in olive oil and apply rub of your choice to chicken inside and out. Reserve 2 tbsp Wickles brine to combine with oil for basting. Place garlic and dill in a jar with remaining brine. Insert jar into chicken cavity and place on kamado grill.

3. Cook for 1.5 hours. After one hour baste every fifteen minutes with brine mixture until finished.

Buffa-que Wings

Servings:16

Cooking Time: 40 Minutes

Ingredients:

- 16 whole chicken wings (about 3-1/2 pounds)
- 1/2 cup Tabasco sauce or your favorite hot sauce
- 1/2 cup fresh lemon juice
- 1/4 cup vegetable oil
- 2 tablespoons Worcestershire sauce
- 4 cloves garlic, minced
- 2 teaspoons coarse salt (kosher or sea)
- 1 teaspoon freshly ground black pepper
- 1-1/2 cups wood chips or chunks (preferably hickory or oak), soaked for 1 hour in water to cover, then drained
- 8 tablespoons (1 stick) salted butter
- 1/2 cup Tabasco sauce or your favorite hot sauce
- 4 ounces Maytag Blue cheese

- 1 cup mayonnaise
- 1/2 cup sour cream
- 1 tablespoon distilled white vinegar
- 1/4 cup minced onion
- 1/2 teaspoon freshly ground black pepper
- Coarse salt (kosher or sea; optional)

Directions:

1. Rinse the chicken wings under cold running water and blot them dry with paper towels. Cut the tips off the wings and discard them (or leave the tips on if you don't mind munching a morsel that's mostly skin and bones.) Cut each wing into 2 pieces through the joint.

2. Make the marinade: Whisk together the hot sauce, lemon juice, oil, Worcestershire sauce, garlic, salt and pepper in a large nonreactive mixing bowl. Stir in the wing pieces and let marinate in the refrigerator, covered, for 4 to 6 hours or as along as overnight, turning the wings several times so that they marinade evenly.

3. Make the mop sauce: Just before setting up the grill, melt the butter in a small saucepan over medium heat and stir in the hot sauce.

4. Toss wood chips or chunks in the kamado grill. Preheat the grill to 350°F using direct heat with a cast iron grate installed.

5. When ready to cook, drain the marinade off the wings and discard the marinade. Brush and oil the grid. Place the wings in the center of the hot grate, over the drip pan and away from the heat, and cover the grill. Cook the wings until the skin is crisp and golden brown and the meat is cooked through, 30 to 40 minutes. During the last 10 minutes, start blasting the wings with some of the mop sauce.

6. Transfer the grilled wings to a shallow bowl or platter and pour the remaining mop sauce over them. Serve with Maytag Blue Cheese Sauce and celery for dipping and of course plenty of paper napkins and cold beer.

7. Press the blue cheese through a sieve into a nonreactive mixing bowl.

8. Whisk in the mayonnaise, sour cream, vinegar, onion, and pepper. It's unlikely you'll need salt (the cheese is quite salty already) but taste for seasoning and add a little if necessary. The blue cheese sauce will keep in the refrigerator, covered, for several days.

Chicken Keema Burgers

Servings: 4

Cooking Time: 12 Minutes

Ingredients:

- 2 lbs ground chicken
- 1/2 cup fresh breadcrumbs
- 1 Tablespoon olive oil
- 2 cloves garlic, finely chopped
- 1 small onion, finely chopped
- 1 egg
- 4 pieces Naan
- 2 Tablespoons Indian Spice Rub
- 1/2 cup Greek style yogurt
- 1/2 cup finely chopped, seeded, cucumber
- 2 Tablespoons chopped fresh cilantro
- 1 tsp finely chopped green onion
- 1/4 tsp ground cumin

Directions:

1. In a small bowl, combine ingredients for the raita and set aside. The raita can be made a day in advance, covered, and refrigerated.

2. In a small skillet, heat olive oil over medium and add onion and garlic. Cook until soft and translucent. Set aside to cool.

3. In a medium bowl, combine ground chicken, bread crumbs, onion mixture, egg, and Indian

Spice Rub until combined. Form 4 patties and return to the fridge to chill for 10 minutes.

4. Grilling:

5. Preheat the grill to 500°F using direct heat with a cast iron grate installed.

6. Place burgers on the grid and close the dome for 3 minutes.

7. Flip burgers and close the dome for 3 more minutes.

8. Close all of the vents and allow the burgers to sit for 5-6 minutes or until the internal temperature reaches 170°F.

9. Serve burgers on naan, topped with raita.

O'neill Williams' Turkey Parmesan

Servings:4
Cooking Time: 35 Minutes

Ingredients:

- 2 egg whites
- 1 Tbsp water
- ½ cup Italian-seasoned dry bread crumbs
- 2 Tbsp freshly grated Parmesan cheese
- 1 lb. boneless turkey breast fillets (chicken can be used)
- 1 cup Italian-flavored tomato sauce
- 1 cup shredded mozzarella cheese

Directions:

1. Preheat the grill to 400°F using direct heat with a cast iron grate installed.

2. In a shallow bowl, beat egg whites with water. In another shallow bowl, combine bread crumbs and Parmesan cheese. Dip turkey into egg whites and then dredge in bread crumb mixture; place in a 13 X 9 pan.

3. Place pan on the cooking grid and bake 30 minutes. Pour tomato sauce evenly over the turkey and top with mozzarella cheese.

4. Bake 5 more minutes or until turkey is cooked through.

Chicken Caprese Stuffed Vidalia Onions

Servings:6
Cooking Time: 60 Minutes

Ingredients:

- 6 large Vidalia onions
- 2 cups diced grilled Springer Mountain Farms Chicken*
- 1 8-ounce package fresh mozzarella pearls
- 1 cup diced fresh tomatoes
- ¼ cup chopped fresh basil
- Salt and pepper

Directions:

1. Preheat the grill to 350°F using direct heat with a cast iron grate installed.

2. Peel and cut ends off onions. Scoop out onions leaving bottom and sides intact.

3. Combine remaining ingredients in a bowl. Scoop mixture into onions, mounding to overfill.

4. Place onions on Lodge cast iron grill and place on preheated grill. Cook 40-60 minutes at 350°F or until tender.

5. Marinate chicken before grilling with oil, fresh garlic, fresh basil and lemon juice.

Italian Turkey Burger

Servings:4

Cooking Time: 10 Minutes

Ingredients:

- 1 pound ground turkey
- 1 (14.5 ounce) can Red Gold Diced Tomatoes With Basil, Garlic & Oregano, drained very well OR
- 1 (14.5 ounce) can Red Gold Petite Diced Tomatoes With Garlic & Olive Oil, drained very well
- 1 egg, beaten
- ¼ cup bread crumbs
- Salt and black pepper to taste

Directions:

1. Combine ground turkey, Red Gold Tomatoes, egg and bread crumbs in a bowl. Form into patties and season with salt and black pepper.
2. Preheat the grill to 450°F using direct heat with a cast iron grate installed.
3. Place on kamado grill and cook to desired temperature.
4. For added flavor put ¼ cup grated Parmesan cheese into the center of each patty.
5. Serve on toasted Italian bread.
6. Top with a thick pasta sauce (heated). Sprinkle with shredded Italian blend cheese.

Greek Chicken Kebabs

Servings: 4

Cooking Time: 15 Minutes

Ingredients:

- 2 lbs boneless, skinless chicken breasts, cut into large chunks (about 2 inches large)
- Wooden Skewers, soaked for 30 minutes (or Metal skewers)
- 1 recipe Greek Marinade
- 6-ounces Greek style yogurt
- 1/2 cup shredded cucumber
- 1/4 tsp fresh oregano
- 1/4 tsp salt
- 1/8 tsp pepper
- 2 cloves garlic, finely chopped

Directions:

1. Place the chicken breast pieces in a large zip top bag. Pour in Green Marinade.
2. Refrigerate the chicken for as little as 30 minutes or up to 4 hours before cooking.
3. Remove the chicken from the fridge. Thread the chicken onto the skewers without overcrowding them, and set aside.
4. Grilling:
5. Preheat the grill to 400°F using direct heat with a cast iron grate installed.
6. Place chicken skewers on the grids and close the dome for 5 minutes.
7. Turn the skewers and replace the dome for an additional 5-7 minutes or until the chicken is cooked through.
8. Meanwhile, combine ingredients for tzatziki sauce in a small bowl. Serve chicken with warmed pita bread and tzatziki sauce.

Pb&j Chicken Satay

Servings:6

Cooking Time: 68 Minutes

Ingredients:

- ¼ cup (60 ml) red pepper jelly
- 1 ½ tsp (8 ml) soy sauce
- ⅛ tsp (1 ml) ground coriander
- Pinch ground ginger
- 1 garlic clove, minced
- 2 lbs (900 g) chicken tenderloins, cut into 1 in (3 cm)
- 3 tbsp (45 ml) natural creamy peanut butter

- 3⁄4 cup (180 ml) canned unsweetened coconut milk (top white part only)
- 2 1⁄2 tsp (12 ml) soy sauce
- 2 tbsp (30 ml) chicken broth
- 1 garlic clove, minced
- 1⁄2 tsp (3 ml) finely grated yellow onion
- 1 1⁄2 tbsp (22 ml) dark brown sugar
- 1 tsp (5 ml) lime juice

Directions:

1. Mix the first five ingredients together in a medium bowl. Spoon a few tablespoons of the marinade in a small bowl and set aside. Skewer the chicken cubes closely together on the Flexible Skewer. Add the skewered chicken to a large resealable bag; add the marinade and refrigerate for 1 to 2 hours.

2. For the peanut sauce, whisk together all of the ingredients in a small bowl. Set aside.

3. Preheat the grill to 400°F using direct heat with a cast iron grate installed.

4. Cook the skewered chicken for 3 to 4 minutes on each side until done. Transfer to a serving plate. Lightly brush the reserved marinade over the chicken; serve the Chicken Satay with the peanut sauce.

Smoky Grilled Chicken Wings

Servings:6
Cooking Time: 25 Minutes

Ingredients:

- Smoked Paprika Chimichurri
- Marinated Chicken Wings
- 2⁄3 cup Arugula Leaves, tightly packed
- 1 2⁄3 cup Garlic Clove, peeled, finely chopped
- 1⁄4 cup Rosemary Leaves, tightly packed
- 2 cup Italian Parsley Leaves, tightly packed
- 2⁄3 cup Shallots, finely diced
- 2 tbsp Sage Leaves, tightly packed
- 1⁄2 cup Oregano Leaves, tightly packed
- 1⁄2 cup Whole Grain Mustard
- 1 2⁄3 cup Extra Virgin Olive Oil
- 2 tbsp Smoked Paprika
- 1 tsp Crushed Red Chili Flakes
- 1⁄2 cup Red Wine Vinegar
- To taste Sea Salt
- 2 2⁄3 cup Water
- 1⁄2 cup White Wine Vinegar
- 2⁄3 cup Lemon Juice
- 2 1⁄2 pounds Chicken Wings
- 1 tbsp Crushed Red Chili Flake
- 1⁄4 cup White Wine Vinegar
- 3⁄4 cup Smoked Paprika Chimichurri
- To taste Fine Sea Salt

Directions:

1. Preheat the grill to 400°F using direct heat with a cast iron grate installed.

2. Place marinated wings on a flat tray and season to taste with sea salt. Place the wings on the kamado grill in a single layer to begin cooking. Allow the skin to begin crisping on one side, then flip and close the lid of the grill to allow the wings to slowly bake as the skin renders crispy. Also closing the lid of the grill will allow the wings to develop that signature smoky flavor that is produced during the cooking process. Maintain a temperature of around 350°F/177°C and check and rotate the wings every 5 minutes to get an even golden brown and crispy skin. The entire process may take anywhere from 20 – 25 minutes. Remove the wings from the heat and place on a wire rack once all the fat is rendered and the skin is evenly crispy and golden brown.

3. Allow to rest for 3 – 5 minutes, then serve.

4. Finely chop all herbs and greens. Combine all finely chopped herbs in a large mixing bowl. Add remainder of the ingredients and mix thoroughly.

Reserve finished chimichurri in the refrigerator until ready for use.

5. On a clean cutting board with a sharp knife separate the drumette, flap, and wing tip; discard the wing tips. In a large bowl combine the vinegar, chimichurri, and red chili flakes. Toss the drumettes and flaps in the chimichurri marinade until well coated and allow to sit in the refrigerator for 3½ – 4 hours.

Blueberry Bbq Chicken

Servings:8

Cooking Time: 50 Minutes

Ingredients:

*   1 to 3 lb (450 g to 1.4 kg) chicken – ask your butcher to butterfly or spatchcock your chicken by cutting the backbone and sternum out and flattening
*   2 tsp (10 ml) salt
*   1½ tsp (8 ml) black pepper
*   3 cups (710 ml) blueberries
*   2 cups (480 ml) apple cider vinegar
*   2 cups (480 ml) granulated sugar
*   1 tsp (5 ml) salt
*   One 3-inch cinnamon stick
*   1 bay leaf
*   ¼ tsp (2 ml) chili flakes

Directions:

1. 30 minutes before you plan to cook it, bring the chicken to room temperature and season it thoroughly with 2 tsp (10 ml) salt and 1½ tsp (8 ml) black pepper.

2. Preheat the grill to 350°F using direct heat with a cast iron grate installed.

3. Place the chicken skin-side up on the cooking grid and roast for 20 minutes, then begin basting with the blueberry sauce every 5 minutes for an additional 20 minutes of cooking. After 40 minutes total, turn the chicken over to caramelize the skin and baste the other side 10 more minutes. Using a thermometer, check the temperature of the thigh. Once it's at 165°F, remove the chicken from the kamado grill and douse the chicken in blueberry sauce; let rest for 10 minutes, then cut the chicken into 6 or 8 pieces and toss once more in sauce. Serve warm or at room temperature.

4. To make the Blue Q Sauce , begin by combining the blueberries and a little of the vinegar in a food processor. Pulse the berries just to break them up. You're not trying to achieve smooth berries at this point; you just want to get some blue juice flowing. In a dutch oven or 4 quart (3.75 L) saucepan, combine all of the sauce ingredients. Bring to a simmer over medium heat and cook for one hour, covered. Give it a stir from time to time to avoid scorching the bottom.

5. Carefully transfer the sauce to a blender. Pull the little knob off the top of the lid and cover it with a dish towel to prevent a mess! Blend the sauce to get it as smooth as you can, then strain it through a fine mesh strainer and transfer it back to your pan. Cook to reduce it by one-third. The Blue Q should coat the back of a spoon and be the viscosity of maple syrup. Refrigerate overnight to let things mellow out. This sauce will keep for months covered in the refrigerator.

Smokey Thai Pulled Chicken Sandwiches

Servings:6

Cooking Time: 92 Minutes

Ingredients:

*   3 lbs boneless skinless chicken thighs
*   1 package of Cobblestone Bread Co.™ Sesame Twist Hamburger Rolls
*   3 tbs chopped cilantro

- quick pickled carrots
- * optional Sriracha sauce
- 3 cups water
- 2 tbs pure cane sugar
- juice of one lime
- 2 tsp Thai fish sauce
- 2 tsp soy sauce
- 1 tbs sea salt
- 1-2 hot peppers (Thai bird or Serrano)
- 2 cloves of garlic
- 1 tbs pure cane sugar
- 2 tsp sea salt
- 1 tsp onion powder
- ½ tsp ground ginger
- ½ tsp garlic powder
- ¼ tsp ground white pepper
- ¼ cup water
- ¼ cup honey
- 1 tbs fresh lime juice
- 2 tbs soy sauce
- 1 tsp Thai fish sauce (add while mixing, do not heat)
- ⅔ pound carrots
- 2½ cups water
- ⅔ cup rice wine vinegar
- 1 tbs pure cane sugar
- 2 tsp sea salt
- 2 tsp fresh grated ginger

Directions:

1. Whisk together ingredients for the brine. Add the chicken thighs, making sure they are fully covered. Place in refrigerator for 2-3 hours.
2. About a half hour before you are ready to grill.Preheat the grill to 280°F using direct heat with a cast iron grate installed.
3. Whisk together the dry rub ingredients. Remove the chicken thighs from brine, and pat dry. Discard brine. Generously coat the chicken with dry rub.
4. Place chicken thighs on the kamado grill. Cook for 1½ hours, flipping once after about 50 minutes. Check temperature occasionally to make sure you are not gout over a maximum of 325°F, damper more narrowly to reduce temperature closer to 280°F.
5. Prepare the Quick Pickled Carrots while the chicken is grilling.
6. When chicken thighs are removed from the kamado grill, set aside to rest and cool a little, then pull the chicken (discard any fatty bits). Mix in chopped fresh cilantro.
7. Mix sauce ingredients, except fish sauce, in a small saucepan over medium-high heat. Once it comes to a boil, reduce to a simmer. Allow to gently bubble for 2 minutes, then shut off and pour over the pulled chicken. Mix. Add fish sauce and mix again.
8. Place some of the pickled matchstick carrots on the bottom half of each Cobblestone Bread Co.™ Sesame Twist Hamburger Roll. Top with a generous helping of the Thai pulled chicken (squirt on a bit of sriracha sauce if you like) and cover with top of the roll.
9. Peel and trim carrots, then matchstick slice.
10. Whisk together pickling brine ingredients in a deep microwave-safe bowl. Microwave for 2 minutes, then whisk again to ensure salt & sugar are dissolved. Add the carrots. Make sure they are fully covered in the brine.
11. Microwave until the brine come to a quick boil (about 5-6 minutes). Microwave for another minute (you may need to stop it a couple times to avoid boil over). Remove from the microwave and set aside to cool.
12. When the brine has cooled to room temperature, drain. Refrigerate the carrots until ready to go on sandwiches.

Green Curry Chicken

Servings: 4
Cooking Time: 40 Minutes

Ingredients:
- 2 lbs boneless skinless chicken breast, cut into 1 inch cubes
- 1 Tablespoon garlic, minced
- 1 Tablespoon ginger, grated
- 2 green onions, chopped
- 2 cups unsweetened coconut milk
- 2 Tablespoon canola oil
- 2 Tablespoon soy sauce
- 2 Tablespoons cornstarch
- 2 Tablespoons Thai green curry paste
- 2 Tablespoons brown sugar
- 1 Tablespoon fish sauce

Directions:
1. Preheat the grill to 500°F using direct heat with a cast iron grate installed with the dutch oven on the grid.
2. Dredge chicken breast pieces in soy sauce, then corn starch.
3. Place oil and chicken in the heated dutch oven and brown. Work in batches, being careful not to overcrowd the pan.
4. Add garlic, ginger, and green onion and stir until fragrant.
5. Add Thai green curry paste, fish sauce, coconut milk, and sugar and stir to combine.
6. Lower the temperature in the grill to 350°F.
7. Cover the dutch oven and the dome and simmer for 25-30 minutes.
8. Serve over jasmine rice with lime wedges and whole cilantro leaves.

Open-faced Leftover Turkey Sandwich

Servings:4
Cooking Time: 14 Minutes

Ingredients:
- Sourdough bread
- 3 tsp butter, separated
- Mashed potatoes
- Stuffing or dressing
- Gravy
- Roasted turkey
- Cranberry chutney or cranberry sauce
- Salt and pepper to taste
- Arugula, optional

Directions:
1. Preheat the grill to 400°F using direct heat with a cast iron grate installed.
2. Melt one tablespoon of butter in the cast iron skillet or plancha and add the mashed potatoes. Once they have a nice crust remove and set aside. Next, add the stuffing with gravy and a tablespoon of butter. Once warmed, about 5-7 minutes, remove and set aside. Lastly, add the turkey with more gravy. Once warmed, about 5-7 minutes, remove and set aside.
3. Toast the bread with a tablespoon of butter and salt and pepper. Then pile on the cranberry chutney or sauce! Next, comes the turkey. Follow it up with the mash potatoes and stuffing. Then drizzle more gravy over. Top with arugula and serve immediately.

Spatchcocked Chicken Two Ways

Servings:4

Cooking Time: 100 Minutes

Ingredients:

- 2 quarts hot water
- 1 cup kosher salt
- 1⅓ cup Sugar in The Raw
- ¼ cup powdered onion
- ¼ cup granulated garlic
- 2 tbsp black pepper
- Ice, enough to bring brine to 1 gallon
- 1 whole chicken about 4 pounds each, cut spatchcock style
- Nashville Hot Seasoning
- 1 whole chicken about 4 pounds each, cut spatchcock style
- Citrus & Herb Seasoning

Directions:

1. One day before the cook, make the brine. In a deep container, combine the water, salt, sugar, granulated onion, granulated garlic, and pepper. Mix well until the salt and sugar are dissolved. Pour the ice into the bowl with the hot brine. Mix well. When the brine has completely cooled, place in the refrigerator for at least 4 hours until well chilled. Use immediately or keep refrigerated for up to a week.

2. At least 12 hours and up to 24 hours before you plan to cook, put the chicken in the brine and weigh it down to keep it completely submerged. Refrigerate until needed.

3. Preheat the grill to 400°F using direct heat with a cast iron grate installed.

4. Remove the chicken from the brine. Rinse thoroughly and dry well with paper towels. Season the chicken on all sides with the Nashville Hot Seasoning.

5. Place the chicken on the cooking grid – meaty side up – and cook for about 15 minutes until well browned on the bottom. Flip the chicken and cook until golden brown on the skin side, about 15 minutes. Flip the chicken again and cook until it reaches an internal temperature of 165°F deep in the breast and 180°F in the thigh. Remove to a platter and tent loosely with foil. Let rest for 5 minutes. Carve to serve.

6. Preheat the grill to 350°F using direct heat with a cast iron grate installed.

7. Remove the chicken from the brine. Rinse thoroughly and dry well with paper towels. Season the chicken on all sides with the Citrus & Herb Seasoning.

8. Place the chicken on the cooking grid meaty side up and cook for about 1 hour and 15 minutes until golden brown and cooked to an internal temperature of 165°F deep in the breast and 180°F in the thigh. Remove to a platter and tent loosely with foil. Let rest for 5 minutes. Carve to serve.

Rotisserie Style Chicken

Servings: 4

Cooking Time: 60 Minutes

Ingredients:

- 1 (4-5 lb) whole chicken
- 1/2 recipe Turkey Brine
- 1 cup White Barbecue Sauce

Directions:

1. Place chicken in Turkey Brine for 2 hours or overnight.

2. Rinse the chicken and pat dry.

3. Grilling:

4. Preheat the grill to 375°F using direct heat with a cast iron grate installed.

5. Place the chicken on the grids, breast side up, and close the dome for 20 minutes.

6. Flip the chicken over and cook for an additional 20 minutes.

7. Baste the chicken with White Barbecue Sauce, flip the chicken, and replace the dome for 5 minutes.

8. Repeat until the internal temperature of the thigh reaches 170°F.

9. Allow the chicken to rest off the heat for 10 minutes before carving.

Braised Chicken Thighs With Mushrooms

Servings: 4
Cooking Time: 60 Minutes

Ingredients:

- 2 lbs chicken thighs, bone in and skin on
- 1 lb mushrooms, thinly sliced
- 1 cup finely chopped onion
- 1 Tablespoon butter
- 1 Tablespoon fresh thyme, chopped
- 1/2 cup white wine
- 1/2 cup chicken broth
- 1/4 cup flour
- 2 Tablespoons olive oil
- Salt and Pepper

Directions:

1. Lightly dredge each chicken thigh in flour and season with salt and pepper.

2. Preheat the grill to 500°F using direct heat with a cast iron grate installed.

3. Place the dutch oven directly on the grid and allow the pot to heat for 5-7 minutes.

4. Pour olive oil into the oven and add chicken thighs, being careful not to crowd the pan.

5. Brown the chicken thighs in batches until they are golden brown on all sides. Remove from the dutch oven and set aside.

6. To the pan, add butter and mushrooms, but do not stir for 2-3 minutes or until the mushrooms begin to brown.

7. Add onions and cook until softened.

8. Return the chicken to the pot and add wine, chicken, broth, and thyme.

9. Cover the dutch oven, reduce the heat of The grill to 350°F and close the dome.

10. Allow the chicken to cook 30-40 minutes or until the internal temperature reaches 170°F. Serve warm.

Walk The Plank Chicken Quarters

Servings: 4
Cooking Time: 60 Minutes

Ingredients:

- 4 chicken leg quarters (drumstick and thigh)
- 4 cups Maple Brine
- 1/4 cup Coffee Spice Barbecue Sauce
- 2 untreated cedar planks

Directions:

1. In a large zip top bag, pour cool Maple Brine over chicken leg quarters and allow them to sit, refrigerated, for 2 hours.

2. Remove the chicken from the brine, pat dry, and allow to come to room temperature while the grill is heating.

3. Grilling:

4. Preheat the grill to 350°F using direct heat with a cast iron grate installed. Place the cedar

planks on the grid for 3 minutes, with the dome closed.

5. Flip the plank and place the chicken on the heated side. Close the dome for 45 minutes to 1 hour or until the thigh registers 170°F.

6. Generously brush the thighs with Coffee Spice Barbecue Sauce and close the dome for an additional 5 minutes. Serve with additional sauce.

Bacon-wrapped Bbq Quail

Servings:12
Cooking Time: 24 Minutes

Ingredients:

- 12 bone in quail halves
- 3 tablespoons Savory Pecan Seasoning
- 1 lb bacon
- 1 cup Vidalia Onion and Sriracha Barbecue Sauce

Directions:

1. Preheat the grill to 350°F using direct heat with a cast iron grate installed.

2. Season each quail half with Savory Pecan Seasoning; wrap each half in a slice of bacon and secure with a toothpick.

3. Grill the quail for 8 to 10 minutes per side or until the bacon is cooked through. When the quail is almost finished, brush with the sauce. Flip the quail and baste the other side. Grill for an additional 3 to 4 minutes to caramelize the glaze.

Grilled Hot Candy Chicken Wings

Servings:4
Cooking Time: 30 Minutes

Ingredients:

- 5 pounds Springer Mountain Farms Chicken Wings split chicken wings, rinsed and dried
- ¼ cup Sweet & Smoky Seasoning
- 2 tbsp seasoned salt
- 2 tbsp cooking oil
- 2 cups Kansas City Style BBQ Sauce
- ½ cup hot sauce
- 1 cup honey
- ½ cup ground cinnamon

Directions:

1. Preheat the grill to 350°F using direct heat with a cast iron grate installed with hickory wood chips. Grill for about 30 minutes or until the internal temperature reached 165°F or higher. Turn the wings occasionally for even cooking.

2. For the dry rub, mix the barbecue rub and seasoned salt into a bowl and blend well. Place the chicken wings in a large resealable plastic bag. Pour in the dry rub and oil, shake to coat the wings well. Marinate overnight in the refrigerator.

3. For the Hot Candy Sauce, mix the ingredients well. Coat the cooked wings with the sauce and serve.

Champagne Quail

Servings:6
Cooking Time: 25 Minutes

Ingredients:

- 12 quail (or chicken breast)
- 2 Tablespoons poultry seasoning
- 12 strips of bacon
- ¾ cup melted butter
- 2 cups champagne

Directions:

1. Preheat the grill to 350°F using direct heat with a cast iron grate installed.

2. Clean the quail and pat dry. Season with poultry seasoning. Wrap bacon around quail; secure with toothpicks. Melt butter in a Drip Pan; add quail and champagne to the pan. Cover pan securely with aluminum foil, place on cooking grid and cook for 20-25 minutes or desired internal temperature is reached.

Chicken All'arrabbiata

Servings: 6
Cooking Time: 60 Minutes

Ingredients:
- 6 leg quarters, cut into drumsticks and thighs
- 6 cloves garlic, diced
- 1 small poblano pepper, finely diced
- 1 large yellow pepper, diced
- 1 large onion, diced
- 1 cup dry white wine
- 3 Tablespoons olive oil
- 2 Tablespoons red wine vinegar
- 1 Tablespoon tomato paste
- 1 1/2 tsp crushed red chile flake
- 1 28-ounce can crushed tomatoes
- 1 bay leaf

Directions:
1. Preheat the grill to 500°F using direct heat with a cast iron grate installed with the dutch oven on the grid.
2. Season chicken on all sides with salt and pepper.
3. Place oil and chicken pieces in the dutch oven. Brown on all sides.
4. Remove chicken and pour off all but 2 Tablespoon of the remaining oil.
5. Add onion, garlic, crushed red chile flake and cook until softened.
6. Add the bell pepper and poblano pepper and cook until softened.
7. Stir in tomato paste and cook for 1-2 minutes or until the tomato paste begins to darken.
8. Add wine and cook for 2 minutes, scraping the bottom of the dutch oven.
9. Add tomatoes, vinegar, and chicken back into the pot.
10. Cover, reduce the heat to 400°F, and close the dome for 35 minutes.
11. Remove the bay leaf and serve.

Lemon Cornish Hens

Servings:6
Cooking Time: 15 Minutes

Ingredients:
- 2 Cornish hens (about 1 3/4 pounds each)
- Olive oil
- 1½ teaspoon sea salt
- 1 teaspoon freshly ground pepper
- 6-8 sprigs fresh thyme
- 4 springs rosemary
- 4 cloves garlic, chopped
- 2 lemons, sliced
- 1½ teaspoon sea salt
- 1 teaspoon freshly ground pepper
- Dripping from pan
- 1 tablespoon unsalted butter
- ½ cup chicken broth
- 1 slice lemon cut in half
- 1 teaspoon fresh thyme, removed from spring
- 1 teaspoon fresh rosemary, removed from spring
- ¼ teaspoon freshly ground pepper

Directions:
1. Preheat the grill to 600°F using direct heat with a cast iron grate installed.
2. While the kamado grill is heating take the Cornish hens out of the package, rinse with cold water and pat dry. Set on a plate or platter.

Drizzle with olive oil and season with salt and pepper. Take 4 springs of thyme and put 2 of each in the cavity of the hen along with 1 rosemary sprig and 1 clove of garlic.

3. Once the kamado grill is at 600ºF, place the dutch oven on the egg and let sit for 5 minutes. Add about 3 tablespoons of olive oil and wait 30 seconds then add the prepared hens breast side down. Cover and adjust the vent to slowly bring the temperature to 400ºF.

4. In about 8 minutes the skin will become very crispy, flip to the other side as the temperature should be at 400ºF by now. Add more lemon slices around the pan and on top of the hens (keep 1 or 2 slices for the pan gravy). Add remaining garlic and a few more sprigs of thyme and rosemary (reserving some for garnish).

5. Cook until the thickest part of the thigh registers to 165ºF on your thermometer.

6. Remove from pan and place on a platter and tent with foil while you make the pan gravy. If you are not making the gravy then let sit for 5-10 minutes before serving.

7. Take any of the large pieces of sprigs, lemon and garlic pieces. Set on your stove top over medium-high heat. Add in butter and once it starts to sizzle take a whisk and scrape up all of the bits in the pan. Add in chicken broth and continue to whisk. Bring to a boil then lower to simmer. Add in lemon slice, fresh thyme, rosemary and pepper. Let simmer for a couple of minutes. Drizzle over the Cornish hens. Delicious!

Smoked Chicken Tortilla Soup

Servings:6
Cooking Time: 40 Minutes

Ingredients:

- 1 tbsp extra virgin olive oil
- 1½ cups diced white onion (one medium sized onion)
- 2 small jalapeños, diced
- 2 cloves garlic, diced
- 1 tbsp chili powder
- 1 tsp cumin
- 1 tsp smoked paprika
- 1 tsp kosher salt
- 1 tsp coarse black pepper
- 4 cups chicken broth
- 4 cups shredded smoked chicken
- 1 15-oz can diced tomatoes (including liquid)
- 1 15-oz can black beans, rinsed
- 1 15-oz can sweet corn (or 1½ cups frozen kernels)
- 1 tbsp chipotle in adobo (a mix of the peppers and sauce)
- 1 lime, juiced (about 2 tablespoons)
- Suggested toppings: fried tortilla strips, jalapeño slices, avocado slices, shredded cheese, lime wedge, cilantro

Directions:

1. Preheat the grill to 400°F using direct heat with a cast iron grate installed.

2. Add olive oil, onions, and jalapeño peppers to the dutch oven and cook to soften, about 5 – 7 minutes. Add garlic and cook an additional 1 minute. Add chili powder, cumin, paprika, salt, and pepper, stir for 30 seconds and allow the dried spices to heat up. Next, stir in the broth, chicken, tomatoes, beans, corn, chipotle in adobo, and lime juice. Stir all the ingredients well and bring to a simmer.

3. Simmer for 20-30 minutes. Add salt to taste. Serve and top with favorite toppings.

Jamaican Jerk Chicken Wings

Servings:4

Cooking Time: 20 Minutes

Ingredients:

- 6 scallions, greens part only
- 1 tablespoon finely minced fresh ginger
- 1 teaspoon ground allspice
- 1 tablespoon fresh thyme
- 1 tablespoon dark brown sugar
- 1⁄2 cup fresh orange juice
- 1⁄4 cup white vinegar
- 1⁄4 cup soy sauce
- 1⁄2 cup olive oil

Directions:

1. Preheat the grill to 350°F using direct heat with a cast iron grate installed.

2. Puree all ingredients in a blender until smooth. Pour over chicken wings. Marinate for about 24 hours. Grill wings until done. Serve hot!

Grilled Duck Breast With Apple Brandy Glaze

Servings:10

Cooking Time: 40 Minutes

Ingredients:

- 4 duck breasts
- 2 tbsp (30 ml) salt
- 2 tbsp (30 ml) black pepper
- 2 tbsp (30 ml) paprika
- 2 chorizo sausage links, meat removed from the casing
- 2 tbsp (30 ml) parsley, chopped
- 3 sage leaves, chopped
- 1½ cups (360 ml) dried cornbread (fresh or bagged)
- ¾ cup (180 ml) chicken stock
- 1½ tbsp (22 ml) extra virgin olive oil
- 1 whole diced shallot or ¼ cup (60 ml) small diced yellow sweet onion
- Salt and pepper, to taste
- ½ cup (120 ml) apple brandy
- 1 cup (240 ml) apple juice
- 2 tbsp (30 ml) sugar
- 1 cup (240 ml) fresh or frozen cranberries
- 1 cup (240 ml) triple sec
- 4 tbsp (60 ml) sugar
- Zest and juice of one medium orange

Directions:

1. Preheat the grill to 375°F using direct heat with a cast iron grate installed.

2. Using a small knife cut a small pocket in each duck breasts, making sure that the pocket goes all the way through the middle of the breast to the other end; do not butterfly the breast. Gently stuff 2 to 4 tbsp (30 to 60 ml) of the chorizo stuffing into each duck breast.

3. Season both sides of the duck with salt, black pepper and paprika. Grill stuffed duck breast, fat side down first, for 8 to 10 minutes on each side until golden brown.

4. Liberally brush glaze on each side of the duck with Apple Brandy Glaze. Let rest on the cutting board for 5 to 7 minutes before cutting; this will allow the juices to distribute evenly and give the duck a resting temperature of 140-145°F for medium doneness. Slice duck breast into ¾ in/2 cm medallions. Serve immediately.

5. Preheat the grill to 350°F using direct heat with a cast iron grate installed.

6. Add olive oil to a Stir-fry & Paella Pan, add chorizo and stir occasionally until cooked through. Add shallot, brown until golden. Add chicken stock and bring to a boil.

7. Remove the Pan from the kamado grill, fold in cornbread, chopped parsley and chopped sage

until well incorporated, and cornbread stuffing is moist. Season to taste with salt and pepper. Allow cornbread-sage stuffing to cool before stuffing duck breasts.

8. Pour all ingredients into a Stir-fry & Paella Pan, whisk together and bring to a boil. Reduce heat to 300°F; simmer until sauce forms a glaze consistency, about 20 minutes. Remove glaze from the kamado grill, allow glaze to cool.

9. In a Stir-fry & Paella Pan, combine triple sec, sugar, orange juice and zest; bring to a boil. Add cranberries and cook until cranberries start to pop. Reduce heat to 300°F, until cranberry-orange sauce turns to sauce/glaze consistency; check for desired sauce sweetness at this point.

Chicken & Veggie Stir-fry

Servings:6
Cooking Time: 10 Minutes

Ingredients:
- 2 tablespoons toasted sesame oil
- 1½ teaspoons plus 1½ teaspoons minced garlic
- 1½ teaspoons plus 1½ teaspoons minced fresh ginger
- 2 pounds boneless, skinless chicken breasts, cubed
- ½ cup rice wine
- ½ cup light soy sauce
- ½ cup chicken stock
- ¼ cup hoisin sauce
- 2 tablespoons rice wine vinegar
- 2 tablespoons granulated sugar
- 2 tablespoons cornstarch
- 1 teaspoon chili garlic sauce (optional)
- ½ cup canola oil
- 4 cups broccoli florets
- 1 cup broccoli stems, trimmed and julienned
- 1 cup julienned carrots
- 1 cup drained water chestnuts, diced
- 1 tablespoon toasted sesame seeds

Directions:
1. Preheat the grill to 500°F using direct heat with a cast iron grate installed.

2. Combine the sesame oil, 1½ teaspoons of the garlic, and 1½ teaspoons of the ginger in a small bowl, add the chicken, and toss to coat. Let the chicken marinate for 30 minutes.

3. To make the sauce, mix the remaining 1½ teaspoons garlic, 1½ teaspoons ginger, rice wine, soy sauce, chicken stock, hoisin sauce, rice wine vinegar, sugar, cornstarch, and chili garlic sauce in a small bowl. Set aside.

4. Place a Carbon Steel Wok on the spander and preheat for 2 minutes.

5. Place the canola oil and chicken in the wok. Close the lid of the kamado grill and cook for 5 to 6 minutes, until seared on all sides. Add the broccoli florets and stems, carrots, and water chestnuts and cook for 2 to 3 minutes, stirring well. Add the sauce and continue to cook until the sauce has thickened. Remove the wok from the kamado grill.

6. Transfer the stir-fry to a bowl and garnish with the sesame seeds.

Matt Barry Wings

Servings:12
Cooking Time: 30 Minutes

Ingredients:
- 3 dozen Springer Mountain Farms Chicken Wings
- 1 cup granulated garlic
- 1 cup kosher salt
- 1 cup white sugar
- 1 tbsp black pepper

- 1 tbsp cayenne
- ¼ cup paprika
- 1 tbsp chili pepper
- 1 tbsp guchang spice
- 1 tbsp bourbon molasses

Directions:

1. Blend spices thoroughly, keep them dry, cool and away from moisture. Toss the wings with an even distribution of spice.

2. Preheat the grill to 375°F using direct heat with a cast iron grate installed. Cook for about 30 minutes, turning occasionally, until the internal temperature reached 165°F or higher.

Rotisserie Chicken

Servings: 6
Cooking Time: 90 Minutes

Ingredients:

- 1 (4-5 lb) whole chicken, gizzards and giblets removed
- 2 quarts warm water
- 1/4 cup kosher salt
- 1/4 cup brown sugar
- 2 Tablespoons whole peppercorns
- 1 lemon, halved
- 2 lbs small waxy potatoes, cut in half (we like Yukon golds)
- 1 lbs carrots, cut into 2 inch chunks
- 1/4 cup butter, softened
- 1 onion, cut into wedges
- 2 sprigs fresh thyme
- 4 whole cloves garlic

Directions:

1. Combine brine ingredients until the salt and sugar dissolve and add enough ice to bring the brine to room temperature.

2. Submerge the chicken into the brine and allow to chill in the refrigerator for a minimum of 2 hours and up to overnight.

3. Remove the chicken from the brine and pat dry.

4. In the bottom of a cold dutch oven, place the vegetables and top with the chicken, breast side up.

5. Gently lift the skin away from the meat and rub butter beneath the skin.

6. Grilling:

7. Preheat the grill to 425°F using direct heat with a cast iron grate installed.

8. Cover the dutch oven and place on the grill. Lower the dome for 1-1 1/2 hours or until the internal temperature of the meatiest part of the thigh registers 160°F

9. Remove the dutch oven from the grill and allow it to sit for an additional 10 minutes before removing the lid.

10. Remove the chicken, place the vegetables on a platter or in a bowl. Carve the chicken and serve.

Farm-fresh Chicken With White Beer

Servings:6
Cooking Time: 45 Minutes

Ingredients:

- 3 potatoes
- 1 fresh corn on the cob
- 1 yellow pepper
- 1 red pepper
- 1/2 green courgette (zucchini)
- 1/2 yellow courgette (summer squash) 4 carrots
- 4 oz (115) Marloeskes (small onions)
- 3 cloves of garlic
- 4 thyme sprigs

- 4 rosemary sprigs
- 1 lb (455 g) peas in the pod
- 1 farm-fresh chicken
- 1 can of white beer
- 2 1⁄2 cups (50 g) arugula
- Olive oil

Directions:

1. Peel the potatoes, cut into chunks and blanch them in lightly salted water. Drain. Clean the corn and boil for approximately 10 minutes in lightly salted water. Drain and slice into thick sections.

2. In the meantime, halve the peppers, remove the seeds and cut into broad strips. Cut the courgettes and carrots into pieces. Peel the Marloeskes and garlic and chop into sections and fine bits respectively. Finely chop the thyme and rosemary and mix all the above ingredients. Sprinkle with olive oil and add salt and pepper to taste. Remove peas from the pod; sprinkle salt and pepper on the chicken and rub with olive oil.

3. Preheat the grill to 350°F using direct heat with a cast iron grate installed.

4. Place a Drip Pan on the cooking grid. Open the can of beer and pour a small layer of beer into the Drip Pan. Place the can in the Beer Can Chicken Rack and put the chicken on top. Position the chicken in the pan and surround it with the vegetables, except the peas. Roast the chicken for about 40 minutes; mix the peas in with the other vegetables and cook about 5 minutes longer, or until the chicken leg reaches a core temperature of 165°F/74°C. Carefully remove the pan with its contents off the grid, cover with foil and set aside.

5. Take the chicken off the Beer Can Chicken Rack and cut off the breasts and legs. Spread the vegetables across a large dish, place the chicken on top and garnish with arugula.

Savory Beer Can Chicken

Servings:4
Cooking Time: 30 Minutes

Ingredients:
- 1 (4 to 5-pound) chicken
- 1 (12-ounce) can beer
- ¼ cup (60 ml) mayonnaise
- 3 Tbsp (45 ml) Savory Pecan Seasoning

Directions:

1. Preheat the grill to 350°F using direct heat with a cast iron grate installed.

2. Pour ½ of the beer into a drip pan. Place the can with the remaining beer in the center of the Folding Beer Can Chicken Roaster and snap the arms into place at the top.

3. Put the rack into the drip pan and place the chicken onto the rack. Combine the mayonnaise and the seasoning and coat the outer skin and inner cavity of the chicken with the mixture.

4. Roast the chicken until the internal temperature reaches 165ºF/74ºC; remove from the kamado grill and let rest for 10 minutes. Carve and serve.

Smoked Brined Turkey

Servings:8
Cooking Time: 15 Minutes

Ingredients:
- 1 gallon water
- ½ cup firmly packed brown sugar
- Rind of 1 navel orange
- 3 sprigs rosemary
- 1 cup kosher salt
- 3 yellow onions, quartered

- 1 garlic head
- 2 lemons, quartered
- 1 turkey, appx. 12 lbs
- 10 sprigs thyme
- 10 sprigs sage
- 3 cups chopped potatoes
- ¼ cup olive oil
- Freshly ground black pepper
- Garlic powder

Directions:

1. BRINE: Pour the water into a large bowl. Add the brown sugar, orange rind, rosemary, salt, two- thirds of the quartered lemons and onions and 1 halved garlic head. Mix until the sugar and salt dissolve.

2. Remove the giblets from inside the turkey and reserve for another use. Rinse the turkey well. Place the turkey in a 2 1/2 gallon resealable plastic bag or any container that is large enough to hold the turkey and the liquid. Pour the brine over the turkey, making sure it's completely covered. Refrigerate for 12 hours, turning occasionally.

3. Soak 2 cups of hickory or pecan chips in water for 1 hour.

4. Preheat the grill to 325°F using direct heat with a cast iron grate installed.

5. Remove the turkey from the brine, rinse well to remove the brining liquid and pat dry with paper towels. Discard the brining liquid and solids. Stuff the turkey with the remaining lemon and onion quarters, the remaining halved garlic head, thyme, sage, and 1 cup potatoes. Brush the turkey with olive oil and season with pepper and garlic powder.

6. Place the turkey on the Roasting Rack in a Drip Pan; scatter the remaining potatoes in the pan and place the pan in the kamado grill. Cook for 12 minutes per pound until the turkey has reached a safe minimum internal temperature of 165°F/74°C throughout the product. If the turkey starts to brown too quickly, carefully tent the turkey with aluminum foil. Reserve the drippings from the drip pan to make gravy.

7. Remove the turkey from the kamado grill and let rest for 15 to 20 minutes. Carve and serve immediately.

Greek Isles Marinated Chicken

Servings:4
Cooking Time: 60 Minutes

Ingredients:

- ¼ cup water
- 2 BOU Chicken Bouillon Cubes
- 1 tbsp Lemon Pepper Seasoning
- 1 tsp Montreal Steak Seasoning
- ½ cup fresh lemon juice
- 1 tbsp oregano, dry
- ½ cup canola oil
- ¼ cup Italian parsley, chopped
- Zest from 1 lemon
- 1 Roasting Chicken (3½ to 3¾ lbs.)
- 3 tbsp oregano leaves, chopped
- 10 oz grape tomatoes, cut in half
- 2 tsp garlic, minced
- ½ cup red onions, sliced thin
- 4 oz crumbled Greek Feta cheese
- 4 oz Kalamata olives, cut in half
- 5 tbsp olive oil
- 2½ tbsp red wine vinegar
- Salt and black pepper to taste
- 5 oz arugula OR Italian parsley

Directions:

1. Combine all ingredients (except for the chicken) in a blender and blend well.

2. Add the chicken breasts to a stainless steel bowl and coat with the marinade. Marinate for 3

to 4 hours under refrigeration; tossing 2 to 3 times during the marinating time. Or place the chicken into a large 2-gallon resealable bag. Pour the marinade into the bag and seal. Shake to coat the chicken and place under refrigeration (repeat 2 to 3 times during the marinating time).

3. Preheat the grill to 350°F using direct heat with a cast iron grate installed.

4. Remove the chicken from the marinade and allow the excess marinade to drain off. Place the chicken onto a Ceramic Vertical Roaster (fill the roaster with a beer or BOU broth); set the roaster into a Roasting & Drip Pan and place on the cooking grid.

5. Cook to an internal temperature of 165°F in the breast and 175°F in the thigh. Serve with Tomato Feta Salad.

6. Combine all ingredients and toss. Do not over-mix. Place into a serving bowl and serve with Greek Isles Chicken.

DESSERTS

Peach Dutch Baby

Servings: 8
Cooking Time: 25 Minutes

Ingredients:
- 8 oz frozen peaches, thawed (or 3 ripe peaches, peeled and sliced)
- 1 cup whole milk
- 4 eggs
- 1 cup flour
- 1/4 cup sugar
- 1/4 cup butter
- 1 tsp vanilla
- 1 tsp cinnamon
- 1/2 tsp salt

Directions:
1. In a blender, combine milk, flour, sugar, vanilla, cinnamon, salt, and eggs until smooth.
2. Grilling:
3. Preheat the grill to 425°F using direct heat with a cast iron grate installed.
4. Place the dutch oven on the grid of the grill and melt the butter.
5. Line the bottom of the pot with peaches and pour over milk and egg mixture.
6. Close the dome for 20 minutes or until the top of the Dutch Baby is golden brown.
7. Serve with a sprinkling of powdered sugar.

Orange Scented Vanilla Cake

Servings: 12
Cooking Time: 30 Minutes

Ingredients:
- 12 oranges
- 1/2 stick of butter
- 1 vanilla cake mix, prepared according to package instructions
- 1/2 lb of powdered sugar

Directions:
1. Cut the tops off of the oranges and, using a spoon, scoop out the insides of the orange. Eat the insides of the orange while you wait for the cake to cook.
2. Pour 1/3 of a cup of batter into each orange, replace the top and wrap with heavy duty aluminum foil.
3. In a separate bowl, combine butter, powdered sugar, and 2 Tablespoon orange juice.
4. When cakes are ready, drizzle some of the glaze over top of each cake and serve inside the orange.
5. Grilling:
6. Place the oranges on a 350°F grill for 30 minutes or until the cake is done.

Peanut Butter Bacon Bars

Servings: 8
Cooking Time: 25 Minutes

Ingredients:
- 1 package peanut butter cookie mix
- 1/2 cup chopped peanuts
- 1/2 cup bacon, cooked and crumbled
- 1/3 cup vegetable oil
- 1 egg
- 1 cup semi-sweet chocolate chips
- 1/2 cup bacon, cooked and crumbled

Directions:
1. Combine cookie mix, vegetable oil, egg, bacon, and peanuts and press into a lined dutch oven.

2. Grilling:

3. Preheat the grill to 350°F using direct heat with a cast iron grate installed.

4. Cover the dutch oven and place on the grid.

5. Lower the dome for 25 minutes.

6. Remove the lid and top with chocolate chips.

7. Replace the cover for 5 minutes until the chocolate chips are melted.

8. Spread the chocolate over the bars to coat them evenly.

9. Top with remaining bacon.

10. Allow the bars to cool before cutting.

Buttermilk Biscuits

Servings: 6
Cooking Time: 15 Minutes

Ingredients:

- 3/4 cups buttermilk
- 1/2 cup butter, cut into 1/2 inch cubes
- 3 cups flour
- 1 1/2 tsp baking powder
- 1/2 tsp salt

Directions:

1. In the bowl of a food processor, combine flour, baking powder, salt and butter and pulse until the butter is the size of small peas.

2. With the food processor going, stream in buttermilk until the dough just comes together.

3. Turn out on a floured surface.

4. Pat the dough to 1/2-inch thickness and fold in half.

5. Pat the dough to 1/2-inch thickness and fold in half again.

6. Pat the dough a third time to 1/2-inch thickness.

7. Using a pizza cutter, cut the dough into 12 square biscuits.

8. Place a sheet of parchment in the bottom of the dutch oven.

9. Place biscuits on the bottom of the dutch oven, being careful that they do not touch. (You may have to do this in two batches.)

10. Grilling:

11. Preheat the grill to 425°F using direct heat with a cast iron grate installed.

12. Cover the dutch oven with the lid and place on the grid.

13. Lower the dome for 12-15 minutes.

14. Biscuits are done when they are golden brown. Serve with butter, honey, or jam.

Sourdough Baguette

Servings: 4
Cooking Time: 25 Minutes

Ingredients:

- cornmeal, for dusting
- for Day 1 (starter)
- 8oz (225g) whole rye flour
- 8oz (235ml) warm water (105°F [41°C])
- for Day 2
- 8oz (225g) bread flour
- for Day 3
- 12oz (340g) bread flour
- 6oz (177ml) warm water (105°F [41°C])
- 8oz (225g) starter
- for Day 4
- 3oz (85g) whole rye flour
- 31oz (915ml) warm water (105°F [41°C])
- 9 1/2oz (270g) starter
- 42oz (1.2kg) bread flour
- 3oz (85g) whole wheat flour
- 1oz (25g) kosher salt

Directions:

1. On Day 1, in a large bowl, combine flour and water, cover tightly with plastic wrap, and let sit

overnight on the counter at warm room temperature, about 70°F (21°C). (Cooler temperatures might inhibit the growth of the starter.)

2. On Day 2, add flour to the starter and mix until a stiff, thick dough forms. Cover tightly with plastic wrap and let sit overnight on the counter at warm room temperature. The dough will rise overnight.

3. On Day 3, in a large bowl, combine flour, water, and 8 ounces (225g) of the starter, and mix until a stiff, thick dough forms. Cover tightly with plastic wrap and let sit overnight on the counter at warm room temperature. The dough will rise overnight and should begin to smell yeasty. (Freeze remaining starter for later use.)

4. On Day 4, preheat the grill to 400°F (204°C) using indirect heat with a standard grate installed and a pizza stone on the grate. In a large bowl, combine rye flour, water, 9½ ounces (270g) of the starter, bread flour, wheat flour, and salt, and mix until a dough forms. Cover tightly with plastic wrap and let sit for 20 minutes on the counter. The dough will continue to smell yeasty. (Freeze remaining starter for later use.)

5. Form the dough into 4 baguette shapes that are 10 to 12 inches (25cm to 30.5cm) long and about 2½ inches (6.25cm) around. Make 3 slits in the top of each loaf to allow steam to escape. Sprinkle the pizza stone with cornmeal and place the loaves on the pizza stone. Close the lid and bake until the bread reaches an internal temperature of 190°F (88°C), about 20 to 25 minutes.

6. Remove the baguettes from the grill, place on a cutting board, and let rest before slicing and serving as desired.

Grilled Fruit Pie

Servings: 8

Cooking Time: 55 Minutes

Ingredients:

- for the crust
- 1 cup all-purpose flour, plus extra for rolling dough
- ½ tsp kosher salt
- ½ cup butter, chilled and cut into small cubes
- ¼ cup ice water
- 2lb (1kg) dried beans, for blind baking
- powdered sugar, for dusting
- whipped cream or ice cream, to serve (optional)
- for the filling
- 1¼lb (565g) seasonal fruit, such as pears and plums, halved and pitted
- ½ cup sugar
- 4 tbsp cornstarch
- 2 tbsp lemon juice

Directions:

1. Preheat the grill to 350°F (177°C) using indirect heat with a standard grate installed. Place fruit on the grate skin side up, keeping them toward the edges of the grate. Close the lid and grill until beginning to soften, about 3 to 5 minutes. Transfer to a cutting board and slice. Set aside.

2. To make the crust, in a food processor, combine flour and salt, pulsing 3 to 4 times. Add butter, and pulse until the texture is mealy, about 5 to 6 times. With the food processor running, slowly add the ice water in 1 tbsp increments until the dough comes together.

3. Turn out the dough onto a floured work surface and sprinkle with flour. Using a rolling pin, roll dough out to a 10- to 11-in (25- to 28-

cm) circle. Carefully transfer the dough to a 9-in (23-cm) metal pie pan, pressing the dough to the edges. Trim any overhang and crimp the edges. Prick the dough with a fork to prevent bubbles during baking. Place the pan in the fridge to chill for 15 minutes.

4. Spread a large piece of parchment paper over the dough and fill the pan with dry beans, pressing them into the edges of the dough. Place the pan on the grate, close the lid, and bake for 10 minutes. Remove the parchment and beans from the pan, and continue baking the crust until golden brown in color, about 10 to 15 minutes more. Remove the pan from the grill and let the crust cool completely before filling.

5. To make the filling, in a large bowl, combine sugar, cornstarch, and juice. Add the grilled fruit and toss lightly to coat. Pour the fruit mixture into the baked crust. Place on the grate, close the lid, and bake until the filling is thickened and bubbling at the edges, about 30 minutes.

6. Remove the pie from the grill and place on a wire rack to cool. Just before serving, sprinkle with powdered sugar. Serve with whipped cream or ice cream (if desired).

Brownies

Servings: 6
Cooking Time: 30 Minutes

Ingredients:
- 1 1/2 cups flour
- 1 cup white sugar
- 1 cup brown sugar
- 3/4 cups cocoa powder
- 1/2 cup butter, melted
- 1/4 cup vegetable oil
- 2 tsp vanilla
- 1 tsp baking powder
- 1/2 tsp salt
- 4 eggs
- 1/2 cup chocolate chips
- 1/2 chip marshmallows

Directions:
1. In a large bowl, combine butter, oil and sugars.
2. Add eggs, one at a time, stirring in between.
3. Add vanilla and stir.
4. Sift together cocoa powder, baking powder, and flour.
5. Add to the butter and egg mixture and stir until just combined.
6. Grilling:
7. Preheat the grill to 350°F using direct heat with a cast iron grate installed.
8. Line the dutch oven with a liner.
9. Pour the batter into the liner.
10. Cover the dutch oven, place on the grid, and lower the dome for 25-30 minutes or until a toothpick inserted into the middle comes out clean.
11. Remove the lid, top the brownies with chocolate chips and marshmallows and replace the lid for 5 minutes until the toppings are melted.

Grilled Watermelon With Honey Yogurt

Servings: 4
Cooking Time: 4 Minutes

Ingredients:
- 1 round of watermelon, 1 inch thick
- 1/2 cup Greek-style yogurt
- 1 Tablespoon honey
- 1/4 tsp vanilla

Directions:

1. Place the watermelon on a 400°F grill with the dome down for 1 minute.
2. Turn the watermelon and lower the dome for an additional minute.
3. Assembly:
4. Cut the watermelon in quarters and place each on a small plate.
5. In a small bowl, combine yogurt, honey, and vanilla and spoon equal amounts over the watermelon. Serve.

Death By Chocolate

Servings: 8
Cooking Time: 60 Minutes

Ingredients:
- 1 chocolate cake mix, prepared according to package directions
- 2 cups chocolate chips
- 1 cup brown sugar
- 1 1/2 cups water
- 1/2 cup cocoa powder
- 1 (10 oz) bag miniature marshmallows

Directions:
1. Prepare cake mix according to package instructions.
2. Line the dutch oven with a liner.
3. In a medium bowl, combine water, brown sugar, and cocoa powder.
4. Pour the mixture into the bottom of the dutch oven.
5. Top with miniature marshmallows
6. Pour prepared cake mix on top.
7. Top with chocolate chips.
8. Grilling:
9. Preheat the grill to 350°F using direct heat with a cast iron grate installed.
10. Place the lid on the dutch oven and set on the grid of the grill.
11. Close the dome for 1 hour.
12. Remove the dutch oven from the grill, uncover, and serve warm.

Grilled Pineapple Sundaes

Servings: 4
Cooking Time: 5 Minutes

Ingredients:
- 4 fresh pineapple spears
- Vanilla Ice Cream
- Jarred Caramel Sauce
- Toasted Coconut

Directions:
1. Place pineapple spears on a 400°F grill and close the dome for 2 minutes.
2. Turn the pineapple and close the dome for another 2 minutes.
3. Turn the pineapple once more and close the dome for another minute.
4. Assembly:
5. Serve pineapple topped with ice cream, caramel sauce, and toasted coconut.

Bread Pudding

Servings: 8
Cooking Time: 60 Minutes

Ingredients:
- 1 1/2 cups milk
- 10 eggs
- 1 loaf French bread, cut into 1 1/2 inch cubes
- 1 1/2 cups sugar
- 1 cup raisins (optional)
- 2 Tablespoons vanilla
- 2 tsp cinnamon
- 1/2 tsp nutmeg
- 1/4 tsp salt

Directions:

1. Line the dutch oven with a liner.

2. Place bread cubes and raisins into the dutch oven.

3. In a large bowl, combine eggs, milk, sugar, vanilla, cinnamon, nutmeg, and salt.

4. Pour the mixture over the bread and raisins.

5. Allow the bread mixture to sit for 30 minutes.

6. Grilling:

7. Preheat the grill to 350°F using direct heat with a cast iron grate installed.

8. Cover the dutch oven, place it on the grid, and lower the dome for 1 hour.

9. Serve the bread pudding with vanilla ice cream or whipped cream.

Whole Apples With Caramel Sauce

Servings: 4
Cooking Time: 60 Minutes

Ingredients:

- 4 Jonathan Apples
- 1 cup packed dark brown sugar
- 1/2 cup half and half
- 4 Tablespoons butter
- 1 tsp vanilla extract

Directions:

1. In a medium saucepan, whisk together the brown sugar, butter, and half and half until melted.

2. Continue whisking 5-7 minutes until the caramel begins to thicken.

3. Add vanilla and set aside to cool before storing in a jar in the fridge.

4. Using a melon baller, scoop the core from the apple.

5. Wrap each apple in aluminum foil.

6. Grilling:

7. Preheat the grill to 225°F using direct heat with a cast iron grate installed for 1 hour.

8. Remove apples from the grill, serve topped with caramel sauce.

Best Banana Bread

Servings: 6
Cooking Time: 40 Minutes

Ingredients:

- 1 cup plain yogurt
- 1/4 cup butter
- 3 very ripe bananas, peeled
- 2 eggs
- 2 cups flour
- 2/3 cups sugar
- 3/4 tsp salt
- 1/2 tsp vanilla extract
- 1/2 tsp baking soda
- 1/4 tsp baking powder

Directions:

1. In a blender, combine bananas, yogurt, sugar, butter, vanilla, and eggs until smooth.

2. In a large bowl, sift together flour, salt, baking powder, and baking soda.

3. Gradually add the wet ingredients into the dry ingredients and gently stir to combine. DO NOT OVER MIX.

4. Line a dutch oven with a liner.

5. Pour batter into the dutch oven and cover.

6. Grilling:

7. Preheat the grill to 350°F using direct heat with a cast iron grate installed and place the dutch oven on the grid.

8. Lower the dome for 30 minutes or until a toothpick inserted into the center comes out clean.

Nutella And Strawberry Pizza

Servings: 8
Cooking Time: 5 Minutes

Ingredients:
- 1 pizza dough
- 1/2 lb sliced strawberries
- 1/4 cup Nutella

Directions:
1. Stretch the pizza dough into a 14 inch round and place it on a pizza peel.
2. Spread the dough with the Nutella and top with strawberries.
3. Grilling:
4. Slide the pizza onto the prepared stone in a 500°F grill and cook for 5 minutes.
5. Remove from the stone with a pizza peel and slice into 8 pieces.

Chocolate Cake

Servings: 12
Cooking Time: 45 Minutes

Ingredients:
- 2 cups all-purpose flour
- 2 cups sugar
- 2⁄3 cup cocoa powder
- 2 tsp baking soda
- 1 tsp baking powder
- 1 tsp kosher salt
- 2 large eggs, at room temperature
- 1 cup buttermilk, at room temperature
- 1 cup strong black coffee, warm
- 1⁄2 cup vegetable oil
- 1 tbsp pure vanilla extract
- flaky sea salt, for topping (optional)
- for the caramel sauce
- 3⁄4 cup sugar
- 4 tbsp water
- 4 tsp light corn syrup
- 1⁄4 cup heavy cream
- 1 tsp pure vanilla extract
- 11⁄2 tbsp unsalted butter
- for the frosting
- 12 tbsp unsalted butter, at room temperature
- 21⁄2 cups powdered sugar
- 1 tsp pure vanilla extract
- 1 tbsp heavy cream
- kosher salt

Directions:
1. Preheat the grill to 350°F (177°C) using indirect heat with a standard grate installed. Grease a 9-in (23-cm) round metal cake pan with nonstick cooking spray and line with parchment paper. (Instead of a cake pan, you can also use a well-seasoned dutch oven.)
2. In a large bowl or the bowl of a stand mixer, sift together flour, sugar, cocoa powder, baking soda, baking powder, and salt. In a separate medium bowl, whisk together eggs, buttermilk, coffee, vegetable oil, and vanilla extract.
3. Gradually add the liquid ingredients to the dry ingredients, stopping to scrape the sides and bottom of the bowl, until just combined. (The batter will be thin.) Pour the batter into the prepared cake pan or dutch oven. Place on the grate, close the grill lid, and bake until a toothpick inserted in the center comes out almost clean, about 25 to 30 minutes. Let sit for 5 minutes, then turn out onto a wire rack to cool completely. (Use a butter knife to loosen the edges if needed.)
4. To make the caramel sauce, in a small saucepan, combine sugar, water, and corn syrup. Place on the stovetop over medium heat, and simmer until the mixture is deep amber in color, about 10 to 15 minutes. Slowly and carefully, add

heavy cream, whisking constantly, then whisk in vanilla, butter, and a pinch of salt.

5. To make the frosting, in the bowl of a stand mixer fitted with the paddle attachment, beat butter on medium speed until light and fluffy, about 2 to 3 minutes. Add sugar, vanilla extract, heavy cream, and a pinch of salt. Beat on low speed until combined, about 1 minute. Increase the speed to medium-high and beat for 6 minutes. Add 1⁄2 cup caramel sauce and mix until combined.

6. Spread the frosting evenly over top and sides of the cooled cake, and drizzle with caramel sauce. Sprinkle with flaky sea salt (if desired) before serving.

Seasonal Fruit Cobbler

Servings: 12
Cooking Time: 90 Minutes

Ingredients:
- 2lb (1kg) seasonal fruit, washed, pitted (if needed), and sliced or halved if needed
- 1⁄2 tsp ground cinnamon
- 2 tsp cornstarch (for juicy fruits; omit for pears or apples)
- 4 tbsp butter, plus more for greasing
- 1⁄2 cup sugar, plus more for sprinkling
- 3⁄4 cup self-rising flour
- 3⁄4 cup whole milk
- whipped cream, to serve

Directions:
1. Preheat the grill to 350°F (177°C) using indirect heat with a standard grate installed. Place the fruit on the grate (or in a cast iron skillet if the fruit might fall through the grate), close the lid, and grill until beginning to soften and char, about 7 to 10 minutes. Remove fruit from the grill and place in a large bowl. Sprinkle cinnamon

and cornstarch (if using) over fruit, and add a little sugar (if desired). Gently toss to coat and set aside.

2. Grease a 9-in (23-cm) grill-safe baking pan with butter. On the stovetop in a small saucepan, heat 4 tbsp butter over medium-low heat until beginning to brown, about 10 to 15 minutes.

3. In a medium bowl, whisk together butter, sugar, flour, and milk. Transfer fruit to the prepared baking pan and spread the batter evenly over top. Place the pan on the grate, close the lid, and bake until golden brown and bubbly, about 1 hour. In the last 10 minutes of cooking, sprinkle a light amount of sugar over top. Remove the cobbler from the grill, and serve warm with whipped cream on top.

Caramel Cinnamon Rolls

Servings: 4
Cooking Time: 30 Minutes

Ingredients:
- 18 frozen cinnamon rolls, thawed (you can also used canned cinnamon rolls)
- 1/2 cup brown sugar
- 1/2 cup graham cracker crumbs
- 1/2 cup caramel ice cream topping
- 1 tsp cinnamon

Directions:
1. Line the dutch oven with a liner.
2. Cut each cinnamon roll into 4 pieces and arrange them around the bottom of the dutch oven.
3. In a separate bowl, combine brown sugar, graham cracker crumbs, and cinnamon.
4. Sprinkle some of the mixture over the layer of cinnamon rolls. Repeat.
5. Grilling:

6. Preheat the grill to 350°F using direct heat with a cast iron grate installed.

7. Cover the dutch oven and place it on the grid of the grill.

8. Lower the dome for 25-30 minutes or until the cinnamon rolls are golden brown.

9. Drizzle caramel ice cream topping over the warm rolls and serve.

4 Ingredient, No Knead Bread

Servings: 4

Cooking Time: 30 Minutes

Ingredients:

- 3 cups warm water
- 1 1/2 Tablespoons yeast
- 1 1/2 Tablespoons salt
- 6 1/2 cups bread flour

Directions:

1. In a 4-quart ice cream container, mix all ingredients until they come together. DO NOT KNEAD.

2. Cover, but do not seal the container and allow it to sit in a warm, dry place until it doubles in size, about 30 minutes.

3. Seal the container and place in the fridge for 1 hour.

4. Place a sheet of parchment paper in the bottom of the dutch oven.

5. Pinch off 1/4 of the dough and form into a ball.

6. Place the ball on the parchment paper and allow it to rest while the grill heats.

7. Grilling:

8. Preheat the grill to 425°F using direct heat with a cast iron grate installed.

9. Score the top of the dough ball with an "X".

10. Cover the dutch oven and place it on the grid of the grill.

11. Lower the Dome for 30 minutes.

12. Remove the bread from the dutch oven and allow it to cool before slicing.

Lemon Poppy Seed Cake

Servings: 10

Cooking Time: 45 Minutes

Ingredients:

- 1 tsp poppy seeds
- 2 lemons, zested and juiced
- 1 vanilla cake mix prepared according to package directions, substituting melted butter for oil and buttermilk for water
- 1 lb powdered sugar
- 4 ounces cream cheese
- 1 stick butter, softened
- 1/2 tsp vanilla
- 1/2 tsp lemon extract
- The juice and zest of 1 lemon

Directions:

1. Prepare cake mix according to package directions, substituting melted butter for the oil and buttermilk for the water.

2. Add the lemon zest, lemon juice, and poppy seeds.

3. Line the dutch oven with a liner.

4. Pour prepare cake mix into the liner and cover.

5. Grilling:

6. Preheat the grill to 350°F using direct heat with a cast iron grate installed.

7. Place the dutch oven on the grid and lower the dome for 30-40 minutes or until a toothpick inserted into the center comes out clean.

8. Meanwhile, combine glaze ingredients, adding milk to thin out the glaze if necessary.

9. Remove the cake from the grill and set aside to cool for 10 minutes before pouring glaze over the cake.

10. Serve warm.

Apple Cake

Servings: 12

Cooking Time: 60 Minutes

Ingredients:

- 2 (21 oz) cans apple pie filling
- 1 (14 oz) jar caramel ice cream topping
- 1 box yellow cake mix, prepared according to package directions and mixed with 2 tsp cinnamon

Directions:

1. Prepare cake according to package directions.
2. Line a dutch oven with a liner.
3. Pour pie filling into the bottom of the dutch oven.
4. Top with caramel ice cream topping.
5. Top with prepared cake mix.
6. Grilling:
7. Preheat the grill to 350°F using direct heat with a cast iron grate installed.
8. Cover the dutch oven and place on the grid of the grill.
9. Lower the dome and cook for 1 hour.
10. Serve warm with whipped cream or ice cream.

Almond Cream Cake

Servings: 16

Cooking Time: 45 Minutes

Ingredients:

- 2 cups butter, softened
- 3 cups sugar
- 6 cups cake flour
- 1 tsp kosher salt
- 4 tsp baking powder
- 2 cups whole milk
- 2 tsp almond extract
- 10 large eggs, whites only
- sliced almonds, to decorate
- for the frosting
- 1 1/4 cups all-purpose flour
- 2 cups whole milk
- 1/2 tsp almond extract
- 1 tbsp vanilla bean paste
- 2 cups butter, softened
- 2 cups sugar

Directions:

1. In the bowl of a stand mixer fitted with the paddle attachment, cream butter until white in appearance. Add sugar and beat until fluffy. In a large bowl, sift together flour, salt, and baking powder. Add the flour mixture to the butter mixture in three stages, alternating with the milk and almond extract and mixing after each addition until just combined.

2. In a large bowl, beat egg whites until they form stiff peaks. Using a spatula, gently fold egg whites into the cake batter, taking care not to overmix.

3. Preheat the grill to 350°F (177°C) using indirect heat with a standard grate installed. Line an 11 x18-in (28 x 46cm) grill-safe baking pan with parchment paper and lightly grease with cooking spray. Pour the batter into the pan, place on the grate, close the lid, and bake until the top springs back when touched, about 27 to 30 minutes.

4. Remove the cake from the grill and place on a wire rack to cool for 10 minutes. Use a knife to loosen the edges, and transfer the cake to a wire rack to cool completely.

5. To make the frosting, on the stovetop in a saucepan over medium-low heat, whisk together flour and milk until mixture thickens to the consistency of mashed potatoes, about 12 to 15 minutes. Stir constantly, and lower the heat if needed. Remove the saucepan from the heat and place in a bowl of ice for 5 to 10 minutes to hasten the cooling process and bring the mixture to room temperature. Once cool, stir in almond extract.

6. In the bowl of a stand mixer, cream together vanilla paste, butter, and sugar until the mixture is light and fluffy and sugar is completely dissolved. Add the flour mixture, and beat until it has the appearance of whipped cream, scraping the sides of the bowl as needed.

7. Spread the frosting evenly over the cooled cake and sprinkle sliced almonds over top to decorate before serving.

Berry Upside-down Cake

Servings: 10
Cooking Time: 30 Minutes

Ingredients:

- 10 tbsp unsalted butter, at room temperature, divided
- 1 cup packed light brown sugar, divided
- 11oz (315g) fresh seasonal berries
- 1 large egg
- 1 tsp pure vanilla extract
- 2/3 cup sour cream
- 11/3 cups all-purpose flour
- 1 tbsp baking powder
- 1/4 tsp baking soda
- 1/2 tsp kosher salt
- 1/4 tsp ground cinnamon
- fresh mint leaves, to garnish
- whipped cream, to serve

Directions:

1. Preheat the grill to 350°F (177°C) using indirect heat with a standard grate installed and a cast iron skillet on the grate. Melt 2 tbsp butter in the skillet and swirl to coat. Remove the skillet from the grill. Sprinkle 1/3 cup brown sugar over butter, pour in berries, and shake the skillet until berries are evenly spread out. Set aside.

2. In the bowl of a stand mixer fitted with the paddle attachment, cream together remaining 8 tbsp butter and 2/3 cup brown sugar until fluffy. Add egg, vanilla, and sour cream, and beat to combine.

3. In a medium bowl, sift together flour, baking powder, baking soda, salt, and cinnamon. Gradually add the dry ingredients to the butter and egg mixture until just incorporated. (The batter will be thick.) Using a rubber spatula, scoop the batter into the skillet, smoothing it over berries.

4. Place the skillet on the grate, close the lid, and bake until golden brown and a cake tester inserted into the middle of the cake comes out clean, about 30 minutes. Remove the skillet from the grill and place on a wire rack to cool for 15 minutes.

5. To serve, flip the cake upside down on a large serving platter and release from the skillet, leaving the berries on top. Garnish with fresh mint leaves, and serve with a dollop of whipped cream.

Upside Down Triple Berry Pie

Servings: 8
Cooking Time: 35 Minutes

Ingredients:

- 6 cups frozen triple berry mix
- 2 Tablespoons lemon juice

- 1 refrigerated pie crust
- 1 cup sugar, divided
- 4 Tablespoons cornstarch

Directions:

1. Place a liner in the dutch oven.
2. In a separate bowl, combine frozen berries with 3/4 cup sugar, cornstarch, and lemon juice.
3. Pour berries into the bottom of the lined dutch oven.
4. Unroll pie crust and place on top of berry mixture.
5. Cut 4 vent holes into the crust.
6. Sprinkle remaining sugar over the pie crust.
7. Grilling:
8. Preheat the grill to 425°F using direct heat with a cast iron grate installed.
9. Cover the dutch oven and place on the grid.
10. Lower the dome for 35 minutes or until the crust is golden and the berry mixture has thickened.
11. Cut the crust as you would any pie.
12. Serve a piece of crust topped with ice cream and a scoop of the thickened berry mixture.

Grilled Sopapillas

Servings: 6
Cooking Time: 18 Minutes

Ingredients:

- 1 pizza dough, divided into 6 pieces
- 3 Tablespoons melted butter
- 1/4 cup sugar
- 1 Tablespoon cinnamon

Directions:

1. Stretch dough into round shape.
2. Place the dough directly on the pizza stone in a 500°F grill.
3. Brush with melted butter and top with cinnamon sugar.

4. Close the dome for 3 minutes, then remove.
5. Repeat with remaining dough.

Chocolate Chip Cookie Peanut Butter Cup S'mores

Servings: 4
Cooking Time: 5 Minutes

Ingredients:

- 8 chocolate chip cookies
- 4 peanut butter cup candies
- 4 marshmallows

Directions:

1. On the grid of a 225°F grill, place one cookie, flat side up, with one peanut butter cup candy and one marshmallow on top.
2. Close the dome for 5 minutes or until the marshmallow begins to puff.
3. Assembly:
4. Close the s'more with the other chocolate chip cookie and get ready for the sugar rush.

Apple Pizza

Servings: 8
Cooking Time: 5 Minutes

Ingredients:

- 1 pizza dough
- 1 cup apple pie filling
- 1/4 cup vanilla cake mix
- 2 Tablespoon melted butter
- Vanilla Ice Cream

Directions:

1. Stretch pizza dough into a 14" round and place on a pizza peel.
2. In a small bowl, combine cake mix and melted butter until it forms a crumbly texture.
3. Spread apple pie filling over pizza dough and top with crumb mixture.

4. Grilling:

5. Bake on a pizza stone in a 500°F grill for 5 minutes.

6. Slice and serve with vanilla frosting.

Grilled Plums With Honey And Ricotta

Servings: 4

Cooking Time: 5 Minutes

Ingredients:

- 4 plums, cut in half and pitted
- 1/2 cup whole milk ricotta cheese
- 2 Tablespoons honey
- 1/4 tsp cracked black pepper

Directions:

1. Place the plums, cut side down on a 400°F grill.

2. Close the dome for 5 minutes.

3. Assembly:

4. Serve the plums, cut side up, with a dollop of ricotta, a drizzle of honey, and a sprinkling of cracked black pepper.

Peaches And Pound Cake

Servings: 6

Cooking Time: 5 Minutes

Ingredients:

- 1/2 cup heavy whipping cream
- 2 Tablespoons sour cream
- 3 peaches, halved and pitted
- 1 store-bought pound cake, cut into 6 slices

Directions:

1. Place the peaches, cut side down, on a 400°F grill.

2. Place the pound cake slices alongside the peaches and close the dome for 2 minutes.

3. Flip the pound cake, and close the dome for an additional 2-3 minutes.

4. Assembly:

5. In a stand mixer, whip the whipping cream until stiff peaks form. Fold in the sour cream to combine.

6. Place a slice of pound cake on a plate, top with a peach half, and a dollop of the cream.

Banana Boats

Servings: 4

Cooking Time: 10 Minutes

Ingredients:

- 4 green bananas
- Chocolate chips
- Miniature marshmallows
- Peanut butter chips
- Crushed cookies

Directions:

1. Split a banana lengthwise from end to end leaving the peel intact on the opposite side.

2. Top with desired toppings.

3. Wrap the banana in heavy duty aluminum foil.

4. Grilling:

5. Preheat the grill to 425°F using direct heat with a cast iron grate installed and close the dome for 10 minutes.

6. Unwrap and serve topped with vanilla ice cream, whipped cream, or by themselves

Fresh Peach Crisp

Servings: 4

Cooking Time: 5 Minutes

Ingredients:

- 2 peaches, halved with pits removed
- Vanilla Ice Cream

- 1 cup good quality granola

Directions:

1. Grilling:

2. Place the peach halves, cut side down, on a 400°F grill and cover with the dome for 5 minutes.

3. Assembly:

4. Remove the peaches and place them, cut side up, in a bowl. Top with vanilla ice cream and granola.

Corn & Jalapeño Focaccia

Servings: 8

Cooking Time: 40 Minutes

Ingredients:

- 2½ cups all-purpose or bread flour
- 1 tbsp kosher salt
- ½ tbsp instant dry yeast
- 1½ cups warm water (105°F [41°C])
- 3 tbsp extra virgin olive oil
- 3 jalapeño peppers, left whole
- 1 ear of corn, shucked
- for the butter
- 1 tbsp olive oil
- 2 tbsp unsalted butter
- 4 garlic cloves, minced
- 2 tsp dried oregano
- ½ tsp red pepper flakes
- kosher salt

Directions:

1. In a large bowl, combine flour, salt, yeast, and water. Cover tightly with plastic wrap, and set aside to rest for at least 8 hours and up to 24 hours. The dough will rise dramatically and fill the bowl.

2. Pour oil into a large cast iron skillet. Transfer the dough to the skillet, turning the dough to coat in oil. Press the dough around the skillet, flattening slightly and spreading to fill the entire bottom. Cover tightly with plastic wrap and let sit at room temperature for 2 hours.

3. After the first hour, preheat the grill to 425°F (218°C) using indirect heat with a standard grate installed. Place jalapeños and corn on the grate near the edges. Close the lid and grill until beginning to soften and char, about 10 to 12 minutes. Cut the kernels from the cob, and seed and dice jalapeños. Set aside.

4. After resting for 2 hours, the dough should mostly fill the skillet. Use your fingertips to firmly press the dough to the edges, popping any large bubbles that appear. Lift the dough at the edges and allow any air bubbles underneath to escape.

5. Evenly scatter corn and jalapeños over the dough, then push down until they're embedded in the dough. Place the skillet on the grate, close the grill lid, and bake until the top is golden brown and the bottom appears golden brown and crisp when lifted at the edge with a spatula, about 16 to 24 minutes.

6. To make the butter, on the stovetop in a small saucepan over medium-low heat, heat oil and butter until butter melts. Add garlic, oregano, and pepper flakes, and cook for 1 minute, stirring constantly. Transfer to a small bowl and season with salt to taste.

7. Transfer the focaccia to a cutting board and brush the butter over top. Allow to cool slightly, slice, and serve with any remaining butter.

S'mores Pizza

Servings: 8
Cooking Time: 5 Minutes

Ingredients:
- 1 pizza dough
- 1/2 cup semi-sweet chocolate chips
- 1/2 cup miniature marshmallows
- 1/4 cup slightly crushed graham crackers

Directions:

1. Stretch dough to a 14" round and place on a pizza peel.
2. Sprinkle dough with chocolate chips, miniature marshmallows, and graham cracker crumbs.
3. Grilling:
4. Slide the pizza onto the prepared stone at 500°F.
5. Cook for 5 minutes, remove from the stone, slice, and serve.

BEEF

Burnt Ends

Servings:4

Cooking Time: 360 Minutes

Ingredients:

- 1 brisket point, about 3 lbs. trimmed
- Olive oil
- Sweet and Smoky Seasoning
- 1 cup Sweet & Smoky Kansas City Barbecue Sauce
- ½ cup beef broth
- 1 cup brown sugar

Directions:

1. Preheat the grill to 275°F using direct heat with a cast iron grate installed.

2. Rub the point lightly with olive oil, then season with the Sweet and Smoky Seasoning. Place in the kamado grill and cook for 4-5 hours until the point is well browned and cooked to an internal temperature of 160°F. Wrap the point in butcher paper and keep cooking. When the internal temperature reaches 190°F remove from the kamado grill and let rest.

3. While the meat is resting, mix together the barbecue sauce, beef broth and brown sugar in the baking dish and place on the grill. Cut the meat into cubes about 1½ inch square. Add the squares of beef to the sauce and toss them well to coat. Cook for 1 hour and check for tenderness. They should be soft to the touch and bite. If they're not done, just cook for another 30-60 minutes until they are. If the sauce begins to dry up just add some additional beef broth.

Easy Beef Calzones

Servings:4

Cooking Time: 12 Minutes

Ingredients:

- 1/2 pound Laura's 92% Lean Ground Beef or 96% Lean Ground Round
- 1/2 cup turkey pepperoni slices, halved
- 1/2 medium onion, chopped
- 1 garlic clove, minced
- 1 teaspoon Italian seasoning
- 1/8 teaspoon salt
- 1/4 teaspoon pepper
- 1 (13.8-ounce) can refrigerated pizza crust dough
- 1 cup shredded reduced-fat mozzarella cheese
- 1 cup marinara sauce, warmed

Directions:

1. Preheat the grill to 450°F using direct heat with a cast iron grate installed.

2. Cook beef and next 3 ingredients on the Half Moon Cast Iron Griddle or dutch oven, stirring until beef crumbles and is no longer pink. Add Italian seasoning, salt and pepper; drain and remove from heat.

3. Divide dough evenly into 4 pieces; pat each dough piece into one square. Spoon beef mixture evenly onto each square, leaving a 1/2-inch border; top evenly with cheese.

4. Fold dough over filling until edges almost meet. Bring bottom edge over top edge; crimp edges of dough with fingers to form a rim. Place on a lightly greased baking sheet coated with cooking spray. Or use our Calzone Press for easy assembly.

5. Place on Baking Stone and bake at 450°F/232°C for 10 to 12 minutes or until lightly browned. Serve topped with marinara sauce.

6. Cooking tip: lightly brush calzones with olive oil before placing in the oven for a nice golden color and crisp texture. These calzones keep well in the fridge for leftovers, too.

Beef Bourguignonne

Servings: 6
Cooking Time: 75 Minutes

Ingredients:

- 2 1/2 lbs beef chuck roast, cut into 1 inch cubes
- 1 lb carrots, cut into 1 inch chunks
- 1 lb fresh mushrooms, thickly sliced
- 8 oz bacon, diced
- 1 tsp fresh thyme
- 2 cloves garlic, minced
- 1 onion, sliced
- 2 cups beef broth
- 1/2 cup sherry
- 1/4 cup flour
- 2 Tablespoons olive oil
- 1 Tablespoon tomato paste
- 1 bottle dry red wine
- Salt & Pepper

Directions:

1. Preheat the grill to 450°F using direct heat with a cast iron grate installed

2. Place bacon in a cold dutch oven and place on the grid with the dome closed for 10 minutes or until the bacon is crisp.

3. Drain the bacon on paper towels.

4. Pat the pieces of chuck roast with paper towels to dry and season with salt and pepper.

5. In the hot bacon fat, begin browning the chuck roast in batches, setting each browned back aside.

6. Drain all fat but 2 Tablespoon from the dutch oven, but reserve it.

7. Add mushrooms and do not move for 5 minutes until they begin to brown. Remove and set aside.

8. Add 2 Tablespoon olive oil to the dutch oven along with 2 Tablespoon of the reserved fat, the carrots, and the sliced onions. Cook until they begin to soften, about 5 minutes.

9. Add tomato paste and cook 1 minute more.

10. Add flour to the pot and cook for 2 minutes.

11. Add back the beef, bacon, and mushrooms and pour in red wine and beef broth.

12. Add thyme and season with salt and pepper.

13. Cover the dutch oven, reduce the heat in the grill to 250°F, and lower the dome for 1 hour.

14. Serve the Beef Bourguignon with crusty bread.

Grilled Meatloaf

Servings: 8
Cooking Time: 70 Minutes

Ingredients:

- 2lb (1kg) ground chuck
- 1lb (450g) ground pork
- 1 cup panko breadcrumbs
- 2 large eggs
- 2 sprigs of fresh thyme, leaves only
- kosher salt and freshly ground black pepper
- 8 bacon slices (not thick cut)
- olive oil
- for the relish
- 1 medium white onion, halved
- 3 red bell peppers, halved
- 2 tbsp extra virgin olive oil

- 3 garlic cloves, minced
- 3 bay leaves
- 3 tomatoes, seeded and finely diced
- 1/3 cup chopped fresh flat-leaf parsley
- 1 cup ketchup
- 41/2 tsp Worcestershire sauce
- kosher salt and freshly ground black pepper

Directions:

1. Preheat the grill to 400°F (204°C) using indirect heat with a cast iron grate and a cast iron skillet installed. Place onion and peppers on the grate (not in the skillet) and grill until beginning to soften and char, about 7 to 10 minutes. Remove the vegetables from the grill, dice the onion, and seed and dice the peppers.

2. To make the relish, in the hot skillet, heat oil until shimmering. Add onion, garlic, and bay leaves, and sauté for 2 to 3 minutes. Add peppers, and sauté for 2 to 3 minutes more, then add the tomatoes. Stir in parsley, ketchup, and Worcestershire sauce. Season with salt and pepper to taste. Simmer for 3 minutes, remove bay leaves, and remove the skillet from the grill. (You should have about 2 cups of relish.)

3. In a large bowl, combine ground beef, ground pork, breadcrumbs, eggs, thyme, and 1/2 cup relish. Season salt and pepper to taste. Form the meat mixture into a 9 x 4in (23 x 10cm) loaf. Lay bacon slices flat on a work surface, overlapping the long edges slightly to form a rectangle. Place the meatloaf crosswise on the bacon and bring the ends of the bacon strips up and around the meat so the meatloaf is fully wrapped in bacon.

4. Place the meatloaf seam side down in the center of the grill, close the lid, and grill until the internal temperature reaches160°F (71°C), about 30 to 45 minutes. Transfer the meatloaf to a serving platter and let cool completely.

5. Cut the cooled meatloaf into thick slices. Brush a small amount of oil on both sides of each slice, return to the grill, close the lid, and grill for 2 to 3 minutes per side. Serve immediately with the remaining relish, warmed on the stovetop (if desired).

Herb-filled Burger

Servings:4
Cooking Time: 8 Minutes

Ingredients:

- 1 pound Laura's 96% Lean Ground Round or 96% Lean Ground Sirloin
- 1 cup mixed herbs (such as basil, parsley, thyme, rosemary), washed, dried, and finely chopped
- 6 tablespoons fat-free cream cheese at room temperature
- 2 teaspoons salt
- 1 teaspoon freshly ground black pepper

Directions:

1. Preheat the grill to 350°F using direct heat with a cast iron grate installed. Lightly oil the grill rack.

2. Divide ground beef into four even portions; divide each portion in half again and pat out into large flat patties. You will have 8 patties.

3. In bowl, mix fresh herbs with cream cheese. Divide the herb-cheese mixture among four of the patties, spreading it almost to the edge of each patty. Top each patty with second patty and seal the edges by pinching them closed.

4. Gently place patties on hot grill. Grill about 4 minutes, then carefully turn and grill another 3 to 4 minutes. Serve alone or on burger buns.

Wine Marinated Beef Skewers With Cherry Bourbon Glaze

Servings:6

Cooking Time: 31 Minutes

Ingredients:

- 1½ lbs (680 g) New York strip steak, cut into 1-inch cubes
- 15 oz (425 g) cremini mushrooms
- 1 large red onion, sliced in large pieces
- 1 pint (480 ml) cherry tomatoes
- ¼ cup (60 ml) beef rub
- 1 cup (240 ml) dry red wine
- ½ cup (120 ml) low-sodium beef broth
- ½ cup (120 ml) diced red onion
- 3 cloves garlic, crushed
- 2 sprigs fresh rosemary
- 8 stems fresh thyme
- 1½ tsp (8 ml) extra-virgin olive oil
- ¼ cup (60 ml) finely diced red onion
- 2 cloves garlic, minced
- 1 cup (240 ml) ketchup
- ¼ cup (60 ml) apple cider vinegar
- ¼ cup (60 ml) bourbon
- ¼ cup (60 ml) cherry jam
- 1 tbsp (15 ml) blackstrap molasses
- 1 tbsp (15 ml) dark brown sugar
- ¼ tsp kosher salt
- ⅛ tsp cayenne pepper
- ⅔ cup (160 ml) kosher salt
- 2 tsp (10 ml) paprika
- ⅔ cup (160 ml) coarse ground pepper
- 1 tsp (5 ml) cayenne pepper
- ⅔ cup (160 ml) granulated garlic

Directions:

1. Remove the stems from the mushrooms, wipe them clean, and cut them in half or quarters based on the size of the mushroom. Place the steak, mushrooms, and onions in the bag of marinade for at least 2 hours or overnight.

2. One hour before cooking, soak the skewers (if wood) in water. Remove the steak, mushrooms and onions from the marinade; discard the marinade. In a large bowl, add the steak, mushrooms, onions, and tomatoes. Sprinkle half of the dry rub into the bowl and mix with your hands. Add the remaining dry rub and mix again to evenly coat. Remove the wooden skewers from the water. To assemble the skewers, start with one tomato, add one mushroom, one onion slice and one steak cube. Use one of each item per small wood skewer for appetizer portions.

3. Preheat the grill to 400°F using direct heat with a cast iron grate installed. Place the skewers on the direct side of the grid, and grill for 3 to 4 minutes until you see grill marks. Flip, then grill for an additional 3 to 4 minutes until you see grill marks. Move the skewers to the indirect heat, apply the glaze liberally to both sides of the skewer and continue cooking until the steak reaches the desired internal temperature. We like to pull at 130°F, or an additional 4 to 6 minutes on indirect heat. As soon as you pull the meat, glaze one last time. Let rest 5 minutes, or until the skewer is cool enough to handle.

4. WINE PAIRING: The char from the grilled steak, savory marinade, and sweet sauce make these excellent pairings for malbec, zinfandel, or even grenache. Stick with a fruity and bold red to stand up to the bold flavors of the meat and cherry glaze.

5. In a 1-gallon resealable bag, combine all of the marinade ingredients.

6. Set the kamado grill for direct cooking without a platesetter at 350°F. In a cast iron

skillet, heat the oil and then add the onion. Sauté for 5 to 7 minutes until the onions are softened but not caramelized. Add the garlic and cook for 1 minute. Add the remaining ingredients and bring to a simmer; this should take roughly 5 minutes. Using an immersion blender, blend the sauce to liquefy the onions and garlic, 1 to 2 minutes. Let the glaze simmer (but not boil) for another 10 minutes. Allow to cool and then store in the refrigerator. (can be made in advance)

7. In a small bowl, combine all of the ingredients. Store in an airtight container for up to 6 months.

Korean Short Ribs

Servings: 4

Cooking Time: 6 Minutes

Ingredients:
- 12 flanken style beef short ribs (about 4 lbs)
- 1 recipe Korean Barbecue Marinade

Directions:

1. Pour the marinade in a large zip top bag. Add short ribs. Seal and let sit in the fridge at least 4 hours, preferably overnight.

2. Remove short ribs from the oven before preheating the grill.

3. Grilling:

4. Preheat the grill to 500°F using direct heat with a cast iron grate installed.

5. Place the ribs directly on the grid and close the dome for 3 minutes.

6. Turn the ribs and cook an additional 2 minutes.

7. Remove the ribs, close all vents to extinguish the fire, and serve.

North African Lamb Shoulder With Tomato Relish

Servings:6

Cooking Time: 180 Minutes

Ingredients:
- 2 tbsp coarse salt
- 2 tbsp black pepper
- 1 tbsp ground cumin
- 1 tbsp sweet paprika
- 1 boneless lamb shoulder, 5 to 6 lbs.
- ½ small sweet onion
- 3 large ripe tomatoes
- ½ tsp cumin
- 3 tbsp cilantro, chopped finely
- 2 tbsp fresh lemon juice
- 3 tbsp extra virgin olive oil
- Salt and pepper to taste

Directions:

1. Preheat the grill to 350°F using direct heat with a cast iron grate installed.

2. Combine the salt, pepper, cumin and paprika. Generously season the lamb with the spice mixture. Roll the lamb shoulder lengthwise into a compact roast and tie with butcher's string at 2-inch intervals.

3. Place the lamb on the cooking grid. Roast until the meat reaches an internal temperature of 180°F, about 3 hours.

4. Transfer the lamb to a cutting board and let it rest for 10 minutes; remove the string. Thinly slice the meat and arrange it on a platter and serve with the tomato relish.

5. While the lamb cooks, grate the onion into a mixing bowl with the coarse side of a box grater. Cut the tomatoes in half width and remove the seeds. Grate the tomatoes into the bowl. Stir in the cumin, cilantro, lemon juice, olive oil, and salt and pepper to taste.

Smoked Beef Birria

Servings:4

Cooking Time: 240 Minutes

Ingredients:

- 8 lbs (3.6 kg) beef short ribs
- 8 guajillo chiles
- 5 ancho chiles
- 10 garlic cloves
- ½ oz (14 g) ginger
- 2 medium onions
- 2 cups (480 ml) water
- 2 tsp (10 ml) freshly ground black pepper
- ½ tsp (3 ml) ground cloves
- ½ tsp (3 ml) oregano
- 8 sprigs thyme
- ½ tsp (3 ml) ground cinnamon
- 4 bay leaves
- 3 tsp (15 ml) salt
- 4 tbsp (60 ml) vinegar

Directions:

1. Preheat the grill to 350°F using direct heat with a cast iron grate installed.

2. Clean the short ribs and marinate in ½ of adobo mix for 2 to 3 hours. Add the short ribs to the grid and smoke for 4 hours. Move the beef ribs to a dutch oven and cover with the remaining adobo; move the dutch oven to the kamado grill and cook for an additional 4 hours.

3. Enjoy with minced onion, cilantro and limes accompanied with tortillas.

4. In a dutch oven, cook chiles, garlic, ginger and onions in a pot with water, until chiles are tender. Drain the water and process together with the rest of the adobo ingredients.

Steak Roll-ups With Porcini Mushroom Rub

Servings:4

Cooking Time: 70 Minutes

Ingredients:

- Coffee grinder or spice mill
- 2 heads garlic
- Olive oil
- Kosher salt and freshly ground black pepper to taste
- 2 portobello mushroom caps, soaked in warm water for 10 minutes
- 1 medium red onion, sliced into 1/2-inch (1 cm) thick rings
- 1/2 cup (125 mL) dried porcini mushroom caps
- 4 beef tenderloin steaks (approx. 8 oz/225 g each), cut 2 inches (5 cm) thick 1/4 cup (60 mL) fresh rosemary, chopped
- 4 strips bacon
- 41/2 tsp (22 mL) butter

Directions:

1. Preheat the grill to 500°F using direct heat with a cast iron grate installed.

2. Cut the tops off the garlic heads, exposing the cloves on the inside. Drizzle with olive oil and season with kosher salt and black pepper. Wrap them in a little bit of aluminum foil and roast for 30–45 minutes, until the cloves are tender. Remove from kamado grill and allow to cool for a few minutes. Squeeze the hot roasted garlic cloves from the heads. Set aside.

3. At the same time as you are roasting the garlic, grill the Portobello mushrooms and red onions for 10–15 minutes, until lightly charred and tender. Remove from kamado grill and allow

to cool. Pat the mushrooms with paper towels to remove excess moisture. Thinly slice and set aside.

4. In a coffee grinder or spice mill, grind the porcini mushroom caps into a coarse powder.

5. Take a steak and stand it up on its side. Starting at the bottom of the steak, make an incision across the steak about ¼ to ½ inch (0.5 to 1 cm) thick and 6 to 8 inches (15 to 20 cm) long. Next slice the steak across and roll it at the same time to cut the beef tenderloin into a long strip of meat about ½ inch (1 cm) thick. Repeat with remaining steaks.

6. Mash the roasted cloves of garlic, mix with a little drizzle of olive oil and season with salt and pepper. Set aside. Lay a strip of steak onto a flat work surface. Season both sides lightly with a little salt and black pepper and a liberal amount of porcini mushroom powder. Spread a little of the roasted garlic mixture across the entire surface of the steak. Sprinkle with some chopped rosemary leaves. Lay a few slices of grilled portobello mushroom and red onion

7. across the entire surface of the steak. Starting at one end, roll up the steak into a tight pinwheel. Take a strip of bacon and twist it up so it looks a little like a piece of bacon rope. Wrap the bacon around the steak roll-up, knot it and secure with a toothpick. Repeat.

8. Again, set the kamado grill for direct cooking at 500°F/260°C.

9. Grill roll-ups for 3–5 minutes per side, until the bacon is crisp and the meat is medium-rare. This is tenderloin, so it won't take too long. Just when the steaks are about done, place a little knob of butter on top of each steak, close lid and let it melt. Remove from grill, remove toothpicks and serve immediately.

Pimento Cheese Burger With Bacon Jam

Servings:4
Cooking Time: 12 Minutes

Ingredients:

- 4 Nature's Own 100% Whole Wheat Buns
- 4 seasoned burger patties
- 1 cup prepared pimento cheese spread
- 1-2 sliced plum tomatoes
- 2 cups romaine lettuce
- ½ cup sweet onion slices
- 1 cup crumbled bacon pieces
- 3 tablespoons maple syrup
- 1 tablespoon balsamic vinegar glaze

Directions:

1. In a food processor, mix the bacon, maple syrup and balsamic glaze until it is fully incorporated to make the bacon jam. It will look like a textured spread, then set aside.

2. Preheat the grill to 400°F using direct heat with a cast iron grate installed.

3. Cook burgers 5-6 minutes per side to desired temperature.

4. Layer bun with burger, pimento cheese, lettuce, onion, tomato and bacon jam. Top burger with bun top and serve.

Smoked Beef Brisket

Servings: 38
Cooking Time: 900 Minutes

Ingredients:

- 1¼ cups sugar
- ⅔ cup ground black pepper
- ⅔ cup seasoned salt
- ⅔ cup kosher salt
- 2½ tbsp ground cayenne pepper

- 15lb (6.8kg) whole beef brisket, trimmed of fat
- pickle slices (optional), to serve
- BBQ sauce (optional), to serve
- to smoke
- post oak, hickory, or mesquite wood chunks

Directions:

1. In a medium bowl, combine sugar, pepper, seasoned salt, kosher salt, and cayenne. Rub brisket with the seasoning mixture. Wrap tightly with plastic wrap and refrigerate for 24 hours.

2. Preheat the grill to 225°F (107°C). Once hot, add the wood chunks, install the heat deflector, place a drip pan on top, and install a standard grate. Remove brisket from the fridge and allow to come to room temperature.

3. Place the brisket fat side up on the grate, close the lid, and smoke until the internal temperature reaches 160°F (71°C), about 5 to 7 hours. Remove brisket from the grill, wrap heavily in aluminum foil, and return to the grill to continue to cook until the internal temperature reaches 185°F (85°C), about 8 hours. (Check the texture of the meat for doneness throughout the cooking process). The total cook time is about 15 hours, or 1 hour per pound (approximately 2 hours per kilogram).

4. Transfer brisket to a serving platter and let rest for 20 minutes. Slice or shred the meat, and serve with pickle slices and BBQ sauce (if desired).

Herbed-up Prime Rib

Servings:8

Cooking Time: 150 Minutes

Ingredients:

- 1 (4-pound) bone-in standing rib roast
- Kosher salt and black pepper

- 4 tablespoons salted butter, at room temperature
- 1 tablespoon finely chopped fresh basil
- 1 tablespoon finely chopped fresh tarragon
- 1 tablespoon finely chopped fresh rosemary

Directions:

1. One hour before you plan to cook, take the roast out of the refrigerator. Preheat the grill to 350°F using direct heat with a cast iron grate installed. Season the roast on all sides with salt and pepper. In a small bowl, combine the butter, basil, tarragon and rosemary and mix well. Spread the herb butter all over the roast, applying the heaviest layer to the fat cap.

2. Place the roast, fat side up, on the kamado grill cooking grid and cook for about 2 hours, or until it reaches an internal temperature deep in the center of 125°F for medium-rare.

3. Transfer the roast to a platter, tent loosely with foil and let rest for at least 20 minutes or up to 30 minutes. Cut the meat away from the bones and slice the roast thickly or thinly against the grain as desired. Separate the leftover beef rib bones and serve them along with the meat.

Cast Iron Seared T-bone Steak

Servings:4

Cooking Time: 15 Minutes

Ingredients:

- 1 large bone-in T-bone steak, at least 2 in (5 cm) thick
- Kosher salt and freshly ground black pepper
- 1/4 cup (60ml) grapeseed or other high smoke-point oil
- 3 tbsp (45g) unsalted butter
- 6 sprigs thyme or rosemary
- 1 large shallot, finely sliced

Directions:

1. Carefully pat the steak dry with a paper towel. Season liberally on all sides, including the edges, with salt and pepper. Let the steak rest at room temperature for 45 minutes.

2. Preheat the grill to 550°F using direct heat with a cast iron grate installed.

3. Add a Cast Iron Skillet to the cooking grid; heat the oil until it shimmers in the skillet. Carefully add the steak and cook, flipping once, until a golden-brown crust starts to develop, about 3 minutes total.

4. Add the butter, herbs and shallot to the skillet and continue to cook, flipping the steak occasionally and basting any light spots with butter. Continue searing and basting until an instant-read thermometer inserted into thickest part of the tenderloin side registers 120–125°F for medium-rare, 6 to 10 minutes total.

5. Transfer the steak to a large platter and pour the juices on top. Let rest 5 to 10 minutes. Carve, serve, enjoy!

Fire Grilled Steak With Steakhouse Butter

Servings:4
Cooking Time: 20 Minutes

Ingredients:
- 1⁄2 cup (120 ml) butter, softened
- 2 tbsp (30 ml) finely minced shallot or red onion
- 1 clove of garlic, finely minced
- 1 tbsp (15 ml) finely minced parsley
- 1 tbsp (15 ml) finely minced fresh thyme
- 2 tbsp (30 ml) of your favorite vinegar
- A sprinkle or two of salt and lots of freshly ground pepper
- 4 thick New York strip loin, sirloin or ribeye steaks
- A sprinkle or two of sea salt and freshly ground pepper on each steak

Directions:
1. Stir all the ingredients together until thoroughly combined. Scoop the butter into a large resealable bag. Press the butter and form a thick log shape, roughly 4 inches (10 cm) long. Tightly roll up the bag, shaping the butter into a perfect round log. Refrigerate or freeze for several hours or overnight until the butter is firm enough to slice.

2. Preheat the grill to 600°F using direct heat with a cast iron grate installed. Just before you begin to cook the steaks, pat them dry and season them heavily with salt and pepper. Position the steaks on the grid at a 45° angle to the grid lines. After a few minutes, turn them 90° to get the perfect steakhouse grill marks. Flip and repeat. Continue cooking until the steaks reach the doneness you prefer. You may press the steaks with your finger to gauge doneness; they stiffen as they cook through. This will take some time to master but it's a skill worth cultivating!

3. Top each steak with a thick slice of steakhouse butter; serve, share and enjoy!

Planked Bison Sliders

Servings:8
Cooking Time: 18 Minutes

Ingredients:
- 1 3⁄4 lb (790 g) bison sirloin
- 1⁄4 lb (115 g) beef fat
- 2 cups (500 mL) caraway Gouda, grated
- 12 small rustic rolls
- 1 cup (250 mL) fresh or frozen blackberries
- 1 ripe pear
- 1⁄4 cup (60 mL) honey
- 1 oz (30 mL) Jim Beam

- 1 spring fresh sage
- Salt and freshly ground black pepper to taste

Directions:

1. To prepare the meat, unwrap the bison sirloin or roast and pat it dry with paper towels. Place bison on a cooling rack over a cookie sheet. Refrigerate for at least 4-6 hours (or even overnight) to allow the meat to air dry. This reduces the moisture in your ground meat and allows for a burger that is not too wet and sloppy; they tend to fall apart.

2. Set up your meat grinder according to the manufacturer's instructions. Cut the bison sirloin into 1- 2- inch (5-10cm) chunks. Chop up the beef fat. Grind the bison meat and the beef fat together. When all the meat has been ground once, give it a quick stir or mix and then grind it again. Place ground meat back into the refrigerator and allow it to rest.

3. To make the Blackberry Whiskey Compote, combine blackberries, pear, honey and whiskey in a small saucepot. Add in the sprig of fresh sage and a grind or two from your pepper mill. Heat over medium to medium-low heat, stirring occasionally, until the mixture reaches a low boil. Simmer for 10-15 minutes, stirring occasionally, until the mixture is slightly thick. Remove from heat, remove and discard spring of sage and season to taste with a little salt. Set aside.

4. Preheat the grill to 400°F using direct heat with a cast iron grate installed. Remove grilling plank from water and pat dry with paper towels.

5. Remove bison from refrigerator. Season the meat liberally with a little salt and black pepper. Scoop the meat (approx. 3 oz/85g) and firmly but gently pack the ground meat into the scoop. Unmold the little ball of meat and place on grilling plank, flat side down. Repeat with all meat. You should be able to get about 12 small balls onto each plank. Squish 'em a little if you must or grab a second plank. Never buy just one, always have a backup!

6. Place plank onto hot grill. Close dome and let bison balls plank cook for about 15-18 minutes, until the burgers are cooked to an internal temperature of 145°F/63°C, medium doneness. You don't want to overcook these burgers as they will get dry and tough. They are much better moist and juicy. Just before the burgers are done, sprinkle the caraway Gouda cheese evenly over top of them. Close dome for a minute or so until the cheese is melted.

7. Warm the rolls, then take one and tear it open. Spoon in a little Blackberry Whiskey Compote and add a burger. Repeat and serve immediately.

Greek Lamb Stuffed Roma Tomatoes

Servings:4
Cooking Time: 7 Minutes

Ingredients:

- Cucumber Salsa
- Stuffing
- 1 Cup (240 ml) Cucumber (Chopped)
- 3 tbsp (45 ml) Onion (Chopped)
- 1 Clove Garlic (Chopped)
- 2 tbsp (30 ml) Dill (Chopped)
- 1 tbsp (15 ml) Greek Yogurt
- 1/2 tsp (3 ml) Lemon Juice
- Pinch of Salt and Ground Black Pepper
- 1 Ib Ground Lamb
- 1/2 Large Onion (Chopped)
- 1 Portobello Mushroom (Chopped)
- 1 Clove Garlic
- 2 tbsp (30 ml) Olive Oil

- 1 tbsp (15 ml) Fresh Oregano
- 1 tbsp (15 ml) Rosemary
- 1/3 Cup (80 ml) Feta Cheese
- Pinch of Salt and Ground Black Pepper

Directions:

1. Combine all of the salsa ingredients and set aside until needed.

2. Preheat the grill to 350°F using direct heat with a cast iron grate installed.

3. Slice off the top of the tomatoes and scoop out the seeds and insides, being careful not to break the skin. Set upside-down on a paper towel to allow juices to run out for 10 minutes.

4. In a Stir Fry & Paella Pan, caramelize the onions. Brown the lamb with the salt and pepper. Add the mushrooms and 3 tablespoons of the tomato and cook for 1 minute. Add most of the feta cheese, reserving some for topping. Cook for 1 minute and remove from heat.

5. Place tomatoes on Grill Rings; fill tomatoes generously. Grill for 5-6 minutes or until tomato skins crack open slightly. Remove from heat, top with cucumber salsa and enjoy!

Donair

Servings:4
Cooking Time: 10 Minutes

Ingredients:

- 4 lbs. lean ground beef
- 1 tsp sea salt
- 1 tsp ground oregano
- 1 tsp garlic powder
- 1 tsp Italian seasoning
- ½ tsp Newfoundland savory (any will do)
- ½ tsp ground black pepper
- ¼ tsp cayenne pepper
- 1 tsp onion powder
- 1 can sweetened condensed milk
- ½ cup white vinegar
- 1 tsp garlic powder
- 4 large pitas
- 8 slices mozzarella cheese
- 2 cups chopped white onions
- 2 cups chopped tomatoes
- 2 cups shredded iceberg lettuce
- 2 cups Tzatziki sauce

Directions:

1. One hour before the cook, place the beef in a large mixing bowl and mix each dry ingredient into the beef until it is coated well. Cover with plastic wrap and refrigerate for one hour minimum to harden and cool.

2. Preheat the grill to 275°F using direct heat with a cast iron grate installed.

3. Gently, add the beef mixture to the skewers by hard hand squeezing it around a skewer. Once the beef is tightly packed on the skewers place back into the refrigerator until ready to cook.

4. Place the beef skewers on the kamado grill and cook for one hour or until beef reaches an internal temperature of 165°F. Remove from the kamado grill and cover with aluminum foil and let rest for 5 minutes. Once cooled, remove the beef from the skewers and shred or chop.

5. Peel back the top section of the aluminum foil and sink your teeth into the best darn wrap you have ever eaten! Other optional toppings include hot sauce, banana peppers, black olives and mushrooms.

6. Slowly mix together the sweetened condensed milk, garlic powder, and vinegar. Add more or less vinegar to reach desired texture. Set aside.

7. Add mozzarella cheese to the pitas and place on the grid for 20 seconds to melt the cheese and warm the pita. Fill the pita with the beef and then add tzatziki, sweet sauce and veggies. Wrap tight with aluminum foil.

Slow Roasted Leg Of Lamb

Servings:6
Cooking Time: 90 Minutes

Ingredients:

- 1 (5 to 6-pound) leg of lamb
- 5 cloves garlic, thinly sliced
- 20 (1-inch) pieces fresh rosemary
- 1/4 cup extra-virgin olive oil
- 1 teaspoon kosher salt
- 1 teaspoon freshly ground black pepper

Directions:

1. Preheat the grill to 300°F using direct heat with a cast iron grate installed.
2. Using a small paring knife, make 20 (1-inch) cuts evenly all over the lamb.
3. Stuff each hole with a slice of garlic and a piece of rosemary. Brush the lamb with the olive oil and season with salt and pepper.
4. Transfer the lamb to the V-Rack and set the V-Rack in the Drip Pan. Put the Drip Pan on the grid and close the lid of the grill. Roast for 2 to 2 1/2 hours, until the instant read thermometer registers 140ºF/60ºC. Remove the pan from the heat and let cool for 10 minutes.
5. Carve the lamb, transfer to a platter, and serve immediately.

Dr. Bbq's Roasted Upside Down Chili

Servings:6
Cooking Time: 120 Minutes

Ingredients:

- 1/4 cup olive oil
- 1 large yellow onion, chopped
- 1 large green pepper, seeded and chopped
- 2 jalapenos, finely chopped
- 4 cloves garlic, crushed
- 1 28-oz can diced tomatoes
- 1 quart beef broth
- 1 cup Vidalia Onion Sriracha Barbecue Sauce
- ⅓ cup chili powder
- 2 tbsp ground cumin
- 1 tbsp brown sugar
- 1 tsp cayenne pepper
- 3 lbs coarse ground beef, formed into a large patty
- 2 15-oz can of dark kidney beans, drained

Directions:

1. Preheat the grill to 350°F using direct heat with a cast iron grate installed.
2. Add a dutch oven (uncovered) to the grid. Add the oil, then add the onion and green pepper and cook until soft. Add the garlic and jalapenos and cook a few more minutes. Add the tomatoes, broth, barbecue sauce, chili powder, cumin, brown sugar and pepper. Mix well and bring to a simmer.
3. Remove the dutch oven and the cooking grid, and then add a couple small chunks of apple wood. Add an grillspander with a platesetter for indirect tiered cooking. Place the dutch oven on the bottom grid and continue cooking.
4. Season the ground beef patty with salt and pepper, and then place the ground beef patty on the top sliding grid, centered over the dutch oven so that the meat drips into the chili. Cook for 1½ hours, adjusting the heat to maintain a simmer.
5. Remove the meat to a sheet pan. Add the beans to the chili and add more water if needed. Break the meat up with tongs and place it in the pot. Cook for another 30 minutes until everything is well blended and slightly thickened.

Beef & Lamb Sliders

Servings: 12

Cooking Time: 15 Minutes

Ingredients:
- 11/2lb (450g) 80% lean ground beef
- 1lb (680g) ground lamb
- kosher salt and freshly ground black pepper
- 1 tbsp dried marjoram
- for the sauce
- 6 cornichon pickles, coarsely chopped
- 4 tbsp coarsely chopped fresh flat-leaf parsley
- 1 tbsp drained capers
- 4 garlic cloves, peeled
- 1 tsp ground cayenne pepper
- 1/2 cup mayonnaise
- 2 tbsp whole grain mustard
- to serve
- 12 slider buns
- 4oz (110g) paneer cheese, cut into 12 thick slices
- 2 large Roma tomatoes, thickly sliced

Directions:

1. To make the sauce, in a food processor, place cornichons, parsley, capers, and garlic, and pulse until finely chopped. Add cayenne, mayonnaise, and mustard, and pulse until blended.

2. In a large bowl, gently combine beef and lamb, and season well with salt and pepper. Add 2 tbsp of the cornichon and caper sauce to the meat, and gently mix. Form the mixture into 12 equally sized patties and make a slight indentation in the center of each with your thumb.

3. Preheat the grill to 400°F (204°C) using direct heat with a cast iron grate installed. Place the bun halves on the grate cut side down and grill for 1 minute. Transfer buns, cut side up, to a work surface, and spread the bottom half of each bun with a spoonful of the remaining cornichon and caper sauce.

4. Place the patties on the grate, close the lid, and grill until charred on the bottom, about 4 minutes. Flip the sliders and grill until the internal temperature reaches 155°F (68°C), about 4 minutes more. Transfer the burgers to the toasted buns and let rest for 5 minutes.

5. Place the paneer slices on the grate and grill until soft, about 2 minutes per side. Top the sliders with grilled paneer and sliced tomatoes. Serve immediately.

Caribbean Stuffed Peppers

Servings:6

Cooking Time: 48 Minutes

Ingredients:
- 6 bell peppers (red, yellow, green, or a combination)
- 2 tablespoons olive oil
- 1 lb ground chuck or ground round
- 1 cup diced red onion
- 2 tbsp minced garlic
- 3 tbsp jerk seasoning
- 1 cup white rice
- 2 cups chicken stock
- 1 (28-ounce) can diced tomatoes, drained
- 4 sprigs thyme
- 2 bay leaves
- 1 (1½-inch) piece peeled fresh ginger
- 1 (15-ounce) can black beans, drained and rinsed
- ½ cup firmly packed chopped fresh cilantro
- ½ cup thinly sliced scallions
- 2 tbsp freshly squeezed lime juice (1 to 2 limes)

- 2 tbsp Habanero Hot Sauce – add more if you like it really spicy!
- ½ cup crumbled cotija cheese (2 ounces)

Directions:

1. Preheat the grill to 350°F using direct heat with a cast iron grate installed.

2. Place the dutch oven on the grid and preheat for 10 minutes.

3. Cut off the tops of the bell peppers and remove the seeds and ribs. If the peppers will not sit upright, cut a thin slice of flesh off the base to level the bottom. Set aside.

4. Pour the olive oil into the dutch oven to heat briefly. Add the ground chuck, onion and garlic. Close the lid of the kamado grill and cook for 3 to 4 minutes, until the meat is browned. Add the jerk seasoning and stir. Close the lid of the kamado grill and continue to cook for 3 to 4 minutes until the ground beef is completely cooked. Add the rice, chicken stock, tomatoes, thyme sprigs, bay leaves and ginger to the dutch oven and stir gently. Place the lid on the dutch oven and close the lid of the grill. Simmer for 15 minutes, or until the rice is cooked and the liquid is absorbed.

5. Remove the dutch oven from the heat and let it sit, covered, for 10 minutes. Remove the lid and, using a fork, gently fluff the rice mixture. Remove and discard the bay leaves and thyme sprigs. Gently stir in the black beans, cilantro, scallion, lime juice and hot sauce (add more if desired). Fill each of the bell peppers with 1 to 1½ cups of the filling.

6. Place the peppers on a Perforated Grid and place the pan on the grid. Close the lid of the kamado grill and cook for 30 minutes, or until the ingredients are thoroughly cooked. Transfer the peppers from the kamado grill to a platter and sprinkle each pepper with cheese. Serve immediately.

Game Day Sliders

Servings:4
Cooking Time: 8 Minutes

Ingredients:
- 1 lb. ground beef
- Salt and pepper to taste
- 8 slices of American cheese
- Your favorite condiments

Directions:

1. Preheat the grill to 450°F using direct heat with a cast iron grate installed.

2. Form the ground beef into 8 equally sized patties, roughly 2 ounces each. Place the patties on an oiled grid and cook for 4 minutes.

3. Flip the patties, top with American cheese and cook for an additional 4 minutes. During the last minute, add the sliced buns to toast them up.

4. Remove the buns, add the patties, top with a pickle and enjoy!

Beef Short Ribs

Servings:4
Cooking Time: 300 Minutes

Ingredients:
- 3-4 lbs. beef short ribs
- Ancho Chili & Coffee Seasoning
- 4 tbsp Habanero Hot Sauce

Directions:

1. Preheat the grill to 250°F using direct heat with a cast iron grate installed.

2. Coat the short ribs with the Habanero hot sauce; the sauce will act as a binder to allow the seasoning to adhere better to the ribs. Apply a liberal amount of Ancho Chile & Coffee

Seasoning to the ribs. Allow the ribs to sit at room temperature for 15 minutes; this will allow the rub to penetrate the ribs and adding the amazing flavors.

3. Smoke the ribs for 5 hours. After 5 hours begin to check the internal temperature; once the internal temperature of the ribs reaches 198°F remove the ribs from the kamado grill and wrap them in butcher paper or foil for at least an hour to allow the moisture to redistribute.

4. Enjoy those ribs; you've worked hard for them!

Frankie Ballard's Rib-eye Steaks

Servings:6
Cooking Time: 10 Minutes

Ingredients:

- 4 bone-in rib-eyes
- Salt and pepper
- 1 tablespoon unsalted butter
- ¼ cup mushrooms, cut to bite size
- ¼ cup chopped leeks
- 1 clove garlic, minced
- ½ cup whiskey
- 2 cups heavy cream
- ⅛ tsp cayenne pepper
- Salt and pepper

Directions:

1. Preheat the grill to 650°F using direct heat with a cast iron grate installed.

2. Coat both sides of the steak with salt and lots of pepper.

3. Set a cast iron skillet or dutch oven on the grid and let it heat up for a few minutes. Add the butter and cook it until it is slightly brown, then add the mushrooms and cook until tender. Stir in the leeks and garlic.

4. Put the steaks on the grid and close the lid. Grill for about 4 minutes for medium-rare, turning once. Move the steaks to plates. Pour the sauce over the steaks and serve – they won't last long!

5. Slowly add the whiskey; it will ignite, so seriously, add it slowly! Once the whiskey burns off, stir and close the lid of the grill. Cook until the whiskey reduces by two-thirds. Add the cream, and stir frequently for 3 to 4 minutes. The sauce will thicken up and will coat a wooden spoon, that's when you know it's ready! Add a little cayenne pepper and then add salt and pepper if you'd like.

Over The Top Chili

Servings:6
Cooking Time: 155 Minutes

Ingredients:

- 2 lbs. lean ground beef
- 2 tbsp Classic Steakhouse Seasoning
- 1 tbsp olive oil
- 1 medium sweet onion, diced
- 1 jalapeno, diced
- 2 cloves garlic, minced
- 1 28 oz. can crushed tomatoes
- 32 oz. beef broth
- 1 10 oz. can fire roasted tomatoes
- 1 chipotle pepper in adobo sauce (minced) + 2 tbsp adobo sauce
- 2 tbsp cumin
- 2 tbsp Ancho Chili & Coffee Seasoning
- 1 tsp cayenne pepper
- 1 tbsp chili powder
- 1 15 oz. can navy beans, drained
- 1 15 oz. can pinto beans, drained
- 1 15 oz. can black beans, drained
- Kosher salt and black pepper, to taste

- Fritos corn chips
- Sour cream
- Shredded cheese

Directions:

1. Preheat the grill to 275°F using direct heat with a cast iron grate installed. Place the dutch oven in the kamado grill to preheat.

2. Mix the Classic Steakhouse Seasoning and beef thoroughly in a bowl and form into a ball and set aside.

3. In the dutch oven, add the olive oil and cook the onion, jalapeno and garlic until translucent, about 5 minutes. Once the onion mixture is ready, add the tomatoes, chipotle pepper and sauce, cumin, Ancho Ancho Chili & Coffee Seasoning, cayenne pepper, and chili powder. Mix all the ingredients together.

4. Add the grillspander Multi-Level Rack to the kamado grill and place the ball of beef on the grid directly above the dutch oven. Cook until the internal temperature of the meat hits 150°F, about 2 hours. Remove the meat from the kamado grill and break into small pieces. Add the beef and the beans to the dutch oven and cook for another 30 minutes or until the beans are heated. Add salt and pepper to taste.

5. Top with Fritos, sour cream and shredded cheese. Enjoy!

Grilled Entrecôte Of Beef

Servings:4
Cooking Time: 20 Minutes

Ingredients:

- Guacamole
- Spice Rub and Entrecote
- Cheesy Tortillas
- 2 Ripe Avocados
- 1 Red Onion, Finely Chopped
- 2 Tomatoes, Inside Removed, then Cubed
- 1/2 Cup (120 ml) Cilantro, Roughly Chopped
- 1 Lemon, Zest and Juice
- 4 Ribeye Steaks
- 2 tbsp (30g) Coarse Salt
- 1 1/2 tbsp (20g) Surgar
- 2 tbsp (15g) Coriander Powder
- 2 tbsp (15g) Paprika
- 2 tbsp (5g) Garlic Flakes
- 1/2 tbsp (5g) Peppercorns
- 2 tbsp (5g) Onion Powder
- 2 tbsp (5g) Fresh Thyme
- 4 Tortillas
- 1/2 Cup (60g) Cheddar Cheese, Grated
- 1/3 Cup (80 ml) Parsley, Roughly Chopped
- Cayenne Pepper
- Lemon Zest

Directions:

1. Preheat the grill to 750°F using direct heat with a cast iron grate installed. Place the steaks on the grill and cook to the desired temperature. While the meat is resting before carving, lower the temperature to 400°F and place the tortillas on the grill, allowing the cheese to melt and the tortillas to get a crust. Cut the tortillas into quarters and serve with the guacamole.

2. Mesh the avocado to desired texture with a fork. Add the rest of the ingredients and mix well. Season to taste.

3. Place all rub ingredients in a mortar and pestle or spice grinder, and grind to just before it becomes fine. Rub generously over the steaks and refrigerate for an hour.

4. Mix all the ingredients and spread evenly over tortillas. Cover with the remaining tortillas and lightly press down. Be careful before braaing as the cheese may fall out.

Chutney-glazed Brisket

Servings:8

Cooking Time: 300 Minutes

Ingredients:

- 1 ½ cups mango chutney
- 1 cup apple cider vinegar
- 1 cup tomato sauce
- ½ cup ketchup
- ½ cup firmly packed brown sugar
- 1 tablespoon Worcestershire sauce
- 1 (6-pound) beef brisket
- 2 cups white vinegar
- ¾ cup Tricolor Pepper Rub
- 2 cups Beer Mop
- 2 tablespoons freshly ground tri-colored peppercorns (black, white, and pink)
- 2 tablespoons sweet paprika
- 2 tablespoons garlic powder
- 2 tablespoons onion powder
- 2 tablespoons kosher salt
- 2 tablespoons dried oregano
- 1 tablespoon chili powder
- 1 teaspoon celery seed
- 2 tablespoons light brown sugar
- 1 cup white vinegar
- 1 cup beer
- ½ cup sliced red onion
- 2 cloves garlic, minced
- 1 tablespoon kosher salt

Directions:

1. Preheat the grill to 225°F using direct heat with a cast iron grate installed.

2. Mix the chutney, apple cider vinegar, tomato sauce, ketchup, brown sugar, and Worcestershire sauce in a medium bowl, until all the ingredients are combined, and set aside. Place the brisket in a large bowl, pour the white vinegar over the brisket, and let the brisket sit for 5 minutes. Transfer the brisket to a rimmed sheet pan and season all over with the pepper rub.

3. Place the brisket on the grid and close the lid of the grill. Cook for 30 minutes, mopping with the beer mop at 15 minutes. Turn the brisket over and close the lid of the grill. Mopping every 15 minutes, cook for another 30 minutes, or until the brisket is brown. Transfer the brisket to a rimmed sheet pan lined with aluminum foil.

4. Using the Grill Gripper and barbecue mitts, carefully remove the grid and add the platesetter.

5. Pour the chutney mixture over the brisket, wrap with the foil, and seal tightly. Place the brisket on the cooking grid and close the lid of the grill. Continue to cook for 4 hours, or until the brisket is very tender. Transfer the brisket to a rimmed sheet pan and let rest for 10 minutes, still in the foil.

6. Remove the foil, slice the brisket against the grain, and place on a platter. Serve immediately.

7. Peppercorns come from berries that grow in clusters on vines. The berries are dried and sold either whole or ground. The most common and recognized peppercorns are black; however, tri-colored peppercorns, which can be found in the spice section of most grocery stores, are used in this rub. If these are not available, substitute black peppercorns.

8. Place all the ingredients in a small bowl. Using a wooden spoon, stir to blend well. Store in an airtight container.

9. You can really get creative with this mop recipe. Lager (light beer) is used here, but for a more pronounced flavor try using a more robust beer. You can also change the flavor by substituting a more exotic, flavored vinegar for

the white vinegar. This mop does great things for Chutney-Glazed Beef Brisket.

10. Using a whisk, combine all the ingredients in a small bowl. If not using immediately, store in an airtight container in the refrigerator for up to 1 week.

Antelope Medallions

Servings: 4
Cooking Time: 15 Minutes

Ingredients:

- 2 antelope tenderloins, 2lb (1kg) in total, cut into 8 medallions
- 4 tbsp olive oil
- for the marinade
- 3½ tsp extra virgin olive oil
- ½ tsp sesame oil
- 2 tbsp brandy
- 1 garlic clove, minced
- ⅛ tsp kosher salt
- ⅛ tsp ground black pepper
- for the sauce
- 1 tbsp olive oil
- 1 shallot, minced
- 1 garlic clove, minced
- ¼ cup brandy
- 1 cup beef stock
- 2 tbsp heavy cream
- 1 tsp hot sauce
- kosher salt and freshly ground black pepper

Directions:

1. To make the marinade, in a large bowl, whisk together olive oil, sesame oil, brandy, garlic, salt, and pepper. Place antelope in the marinade, cover with plastic wrap, and refrigerate for 2 hours.

2. Preheat the grill to 400°F (204°C) using direct heat with a cast iron grate installed and a cast iron skillet on the grate. Remove the medallions from the marinade, pat dry with paper towels, and coat with olive oil on all sides. Place the medallions on the grate (not in the skillet), close the lid, and grill until the internal temperature reaches 160°F (71°C), about 3 to 5 minutes per side, flipping once.

3. To make the sauce, in the hot skillet, heat oil until shimmering. Add shallot and garlic, and sauté until they begin to brown, about 2 minutes. Add brandy and flambé. (The heat of the pan should create a burst of flame.) When the flames subside, add stock, cream, and hot sauce. Close the lid and cook until the sauce has reduced to ¼ cup, about 5 to 8 minutes.

4. Remove the medallions from the grill, spoon sauce over top, and serve immediately.

Hoisin Grilled Rabbit

Servings: 8
Cooking Time: 25 Minutes

Ingredients:

- 2 rabbits, about 4lb (1.8kg) in total, quartered
- ¼ cup hoisin sauce
- for the brine
- ⅔ cup kosher salt
- ⅔ cup packed light brown sugar
- 4 tbsp pickling spice
- 8 cups hot water
- 2 tbsp Chinese five-spice powder
- for the pickled carrots
- ¼ cup sugar
- ½ cup rice vinegar
- ½ cup water
- 2 tbsp hot sauce
- 2lb (1kg) carrots, peeled
- for the succotash
- 1 red bell pepper, left whole

- 2 ears of corn, shucked
- 2 tbsp extra virgin olive oil
- 1 cup diced red onion
- 1 large garlic clove, minced
- 1 cup fresh edamame, shelled
- kosher salt and freshly ground black pepper
- 1 tbsp thinly sliced fresh basil

Directions:

1. To make the brine, in a large bowl, whisk together salt, brown sugar, pickling spice, and water until salt and sugar have dissolved. Add ice cubes a few at a time until the liquid is no longer hot. Stir in Chinese five-spice powder. Place rabbit pieces in a large resealable plastic bag and add brine to fully cover. (Any extra brine can be refrigerated and saved for a later use.) Refrigerate for 1 hour.

2. Preheat the grill to 325°F (163°C) using direct heat with a cast iron grate installed. Place carrots, pepper, and corn on the grate, close the lid, and grill until beginning to soften and char, about 6 to 8 minutes. Remove the vegetables from the grill, place a dutch oven on the grate to heat, and close the lid. Once the vegetables are cool enough to handle, cut the kernels from the cobs, seed and dice pepper, and slice carrots into rounds.

3. To make the pickled carrots, in a small saucepan, combine sugar, vinegar, and water. Place on the stovetop over high heat and bring to a boil. Reduce heat to low and stir in the hot sauce. Remove from the heat. Pack the sliced carrots into several airtight containers and pour the hot pickling solution over the carrots to cover. Cover the containers with lids, let cool to room temperature, and refrigerate for at least 2 hours before using. (Pickled carrots can be made in advance and will keep for up to 6 months in the fridge.)

4. Remove rabbit from the brine and pat dry with paper towels. Lightly brush with hoisin sauce and place on the grate next to the dutch oven. To the dutch oven, add oil, onion, garlic, edamame, and grilled pepper and corn. Leave the dutch oven uncovered, close the grill lid, and grill rabbit until the meat reaches an internal temperature of 160°F (71°C) and the onions are soft, about 10 to 15 minutes, turning the rabbit pieces once. Season the succotash with salt and pepper to taste and sprinkle with basil.

5. Remove rabbit and the dutch oven from the grill and serve immediately with the pickled carrots.

Red Gold Spicy Burgers

Servings: 4
Cooking Time: 12 Minutes

Ingredients:

- 1 pound lean ground beef
- 1 (14.5 ounce) can Red Gold Petite Diced Tomatoes with Green Chilies, drained very well
- Salt and black pepper to taste
- For an added kick add a slice of pepper jack cheese into the center of each patty.
- Serve on toasted bun
- Top with Red Gold Mama Selita's Jalapeno Ketchup or Chipotle Mayo
- Top with slices of spicy peppers

Directions:

1. Preheat the grill to 400°F using direct heat with a cast iron grate installed.

2. Combine the ground beef and Red Gold Petite Diced Tomatoes with Green Chilies in a bowl. Form into patties and season with salt and black pepper.

3. Place directly on the cooking grid and cook for 5-6 minutes per side to desired temperature (160°F for completely cooked burgers).

Smoked & Braised Beef Chuck Steak

Servings: 8
Cooking Time: 210 Minutes

Ingredients:

- 2½lb (1.2kg) thick-cut chuck steak
- 1 large yellow onion, halved
- 1 green bell pepper, halved
- 4 tbsp extra virgin olive oil
- 4 garlic cloves, smashed
- 4 carrots, cut into ½-in (1.25-cm) pieces
- 3 celery stalks, cut into 1-in (2.5-cm) pieces
- peels of 2 oranges, thinly sliced
- ½ cup fruity red wine
- 2½ cups beef or chicken stock
- kosher salt and freshly ground black pepper
- for the rub
- ¼ cup kosher salt
- 4 tbsp ground black pepper
- 2 tbsp garlic salt
- 1 tbsp paprika
- 1 tbsp ground cayenne pepper
- ¼ cup raw sugar
- to smoke
- post oak, wine barrel, or grapevine wood chunks

Directions:

1. To make the rub, in a small bowl, combine all the rub ingredients. Rub spice mixture all over steak to ensure even and full coverage. Wrap tightly with plastic wrap and refrigerate for 4 to 24 hours. Before smoking, remove steak from the fridge and allow to come to room temperature.

2. Preheat the grill to 350°F (177°C). Once hot, add the wood chunks and install the heat deflector and a drip pan. Install a cast iron grate with a dutch oven on the grate. Place onion and pepper on the grate, close the lid, and grill until beginning to soften and char, about 7 to 10 minutes. Transfer onion and pepper to a cutting board and thinly slice. Set aside.

3. Place steak on the grate, close the lid, and smoke until the internal temperature reaches 190°F (88°C), about 45 minutes. Remove steak from the grill and let rest for 10 to 15 minutes. (Cut into large pieces for braising if needed.)

4. To braise the meat, heat oil in the dutch oven until shimmering. Add the smoked steak and the grilled onion and pepper to the dutch oven along with garlic, carrots, celery, orange peels, wine, and stock. (Steak should be fully submerged in liquid). Leaving the dutch oven uncovered, close the grill lid and cook until steak is tender, about 2½ hours, turning once halfway through.

5. Transfer steak to a cutting board, thickly slice across the grain, and arrange on a large serving platter along with some of the braised vegetables. Skim any fat from the braising liquid and spoon some of the liquid over the steak and vegetables. Season with salt and pepper to taste. Serve immediately.

Italian Meatballs

Servings: 12
Cooking Time: 30 Minutes

Ingredients:

- ¼ cup panko breadcrumbs, lightly toasted
- ¾lb (340g) Roma tomatoes, peeled and chopped
- 2 tbsp extra virgin olive oil, divided
- ½ tbsp nonpareil capers, drained and chopped
- ½ tsp dried oregano
- ½ tsp dried marjoram

- 1 tbsp fresh basil, plus more for serving, chopped
- 1/3 lb (150g) ground pork
- 1/3 lb (150g) ground beef
- 1/3 lb (150g) ground veal
- 3 tsp whole milk
- 1 large egg, lightly beaten
- 2 pitted Kalamata olives, minced
- 1 tbsp grated Parmesan cheese, plus more for serving
- 1 tbsp fresh flat-leaf parsley, minced
- 1 tsp kosher salt, plus more as needed
- freshly ground black pepper

Directions:

1. Preheat the grill to 375°F (191°C) using indirect heat with a standard grate and a cast iron skillet installed.

2. On a rimmed sheet pan, place breadcrumbs in a single layer and toast until beginning to brown, about 3 to 5 minutes. Remove the pan from the grill and set aside.

3. Place tomatoes in a food processor and purée. Place tomatoes and 1 tbsp oil in the skillet. Bring to a boil, slightly close the top and bottom vents to reduce the temperature to 325°F (163°C), close the lid, and simmer until the sauce starts to thicken, about 5 minutes, stirring occasionally.

4. Add capers, oregano, and marjoram to the skillet, and simmer until the sauce has reduced to 1 1/4 cups, about 5 minutes. Add basil, season with salt to taste, and set aside.

5. In a large bowl, combine pork, beef, and veal. Add breadcrumbs, milk, egg, olives, Parmesan cheese, parsley, and salt, and mix well with your hands. Shape the mixture into 12 meatballs.

6. Slightly open the top and bottom vents to return the temperature to 375°F (191°C). Once the grill reaches the needed temperature, return the skillet to the grill and heat the remaining 1 tbsp oil until shimmering. Place the meatballs in the skillet, close the lid, and cook until they start to brown, about 8 minutes, turning once every 2 minutes. Add the sauce, close the lid, and cook until the meatballs are cooked through and the sauce is hot, about 8 minutes.

7. Remove the meatballs from the grill, place on a large serving platter, and top with more Parmesan cheese and basil. Serve immediately.

PORK

Bourbon Grilled Pork Chops With Peach Barbecue Sauce

Servings:4
Cooking Time: 35 Minutes

Ingredients:
- 4 peaches (about 1¼ pounds), halved, pitted, and quartered
- 2 medium ripe tomatoes, seeded and quartered
- 1 tablespoon canola oil
- 1 sweet onion, chopped
- 1 tablespoon finely chopped fresh ginger
- ¼ cup apple cider vinegar
- ¼ cup honey
- 2 tablespoons bourbon
- ¼ cup coarse kosher salt, plus more for seasoning
- Freshly ground black pepper
- ¼ cup firmly packed brown sugar
- 2 cups boiling water
- 3 cups ice cubes
- 4 center cut, bone-in pork chops, about 1-inch thick, well trimmed (2¾ to 3 pounds)

Directions:
1. In the bowl of a food processor fitted with the metal blade, puree the peaches and tomatoes until smooth; set aside. Heat the oil in a medium saucepan over medium-high heat until shimmering. Add the onion and cook, stirring occasionally, until golden brown, 5 to 7 minutes. Add the ginger and cook, stirring frequently, until fragrant, 1 to 2 minutes. Add the reserved peach-tomato puree, vinegar, honey, and bourbon; season with salt and pepper. Bring the mixture to a boil over high heat, then decrease the heat to simmer. Cook until the mixture is reduced by half and thickened, about 20 minutes. Taste and adjust for the seasoning with salt and pepper. Reserve ¼ cup sauce for basting the chops, and keep the remaining sauce warm in the saucepan until ready to serve.

2. Meanwhile, place the remaining ¼ cup salt and brown sugar in a medium heatproof bowl. Pour over the 2 cups boiling water and stir to dissolve. Add the ice cubes and stir to cool. Add the pork chops, cover the bowl with plastic wrap, and refrigerate to marinate, about 30 minutes. (Do not marinate any longer or the pork will be too salty. If you can't cook it right at the 30-minute mark, remove the pork from the marinade and refrigerate until ready to continue.) Remove from the brine, rinse well, and thoroughly dry pat with paper towels. Set aside.

3. Season the pork chops with pepper. Preheat the grill to 400°F using direct heat with a cast iron grate installed. Place the pork chops on the cooking grid for 3 to 5 minutes per side or until the internal temperature reaches 145°F, brushing with Peach Barbecue Sauce in the last few minutes. Remove to a plate and cover with aluminum foil to rest and let the juices redistribute, 3 to 5 minutes. Serve immediately with reserved warm sauce on the side.

Grilled Tequila Chicken

Servings: 12
Cooking Time: 65 Minutes

Ingredients:

- 12 skinless, boneless chicken thighs, about 3lb (1.4kg) in total
- for the marinade
- juice of 4 limes
- 1/4 cup olive oil
- 1 cup tequila
- 2 tsp kosher salt
- 5 garlic cloves
- 1 jalapeño pepper, sliced
- 1/2 bunch of fresh cilantro, chopped
- for the salad
- 1 cup dried black beans
- 1/4 cup tequila
- 2 cups vegetable stock
- 2 Roma tomatoes, diced
- 1/4 cup diced orange bell pepper
- 1/4 cup diced yellow onion
- 1/4 cup diced scallions
- 1/4 cup diced mango
- 1 tbsp chopped fresh cilantro
- 1 jalapeño pepper, seeded and minced
- 4 tbsp sherry vinegar
- juice of 1 lime
- 3 tbsp honey
- 1 tbsp kosher salt
- 1 tsp ground black pepper
- pinch of ground cumin
- 4 ears of corn, shucked

Directions:

1. To make the marinade, add all the marinade ingredients to a food processor and pulse until well combined. Place chicken thighs in a large resealable plastic bag and pour in the marinade mixture. Refrigerate for at least 2 hours or overnight.

2. Place black beans in a medium bowl and add tequila to cover. Cover with plastic wrap and refrigerate overnight. Drain beans and place in a saucepan on the stovetop. Add vegetable stock to cover by 1 inch (5cm) and bring to a boil. Reduce heat to a simmer, cover, and cook until beans are tender but not falling apart, about 30 to 45 minutes.

3. Drain beans and place in a large bowl. Add tomatoes, pepper, onion, scallions, mango, cilantro, jalapeño, vinegar, lime juice, honey, salt, pepper, and cumin. Stir gently until all ingredients are well mixed. Cover and refrigerate for at least 1 hour to allow the flavors to meld.

4. Preheat the grill to 425°F (218°C) using direct heat with a cast iron grate installed. Place corn on the grate and grill until lightly charred, about 6 to 8 minutes. Transfer the corn to a cutting board and cut the kernels from the cobs. Stir kernels into the black bean salad and set aside.

5. Remove chicken thighs from the marinade and place on the grate (discarding the marinade). Close the lid and grill until the internal temperature reaches 165°F (74°C), about 4 to 5 minutes per side, turning only once. Remove thighs from the grill, slice, and serve over the corn and black bean salad.

Skewered Balinese Chicken

Servings: 8
Cooking Time: 10 Minutes

Ingredients:

- 10 garlic cloves, peeled
- 3 fresh cayenne peppers, halved and seeded
- 3 small shallots, halved
- 2 fresh bay leaves

- 1 tbsp chopped fresh ginger
- 1 tsp ground turmeric
- 4 tbsp vegetable oil, divided
- kosher salt and freshly ground black pepper
- 2lb (1kg) chicken breast, trimmed and cut into 1/2-in (1.25-cm) strips
- 4 limes, halved, to serve

Directions:

1. In a food processor, combine garlic, peppers, shallots, bay leaves, ginger, and turmeric. Pulse until finely chopped. Add 3 tbsp oil and pulse until the mixture forms a paste-like consistency.

2. In a sauté pan on the stovetop, heat remaining 1 tbsp oil over medium heat until shimmering. Add the spice paste, and cook until fragrant and lightly browned, about 5 minutes, stirring often. Remove the skillet from the heat, let the paste cool completely, and season with salt and pepper to taste.

3. Skewer the strips, place in a baking dish, and rub with the paste until thoroughly coated. Cover with plastic wrap and refrigerate for 4 hours or overnight.

4. Preheat the grill to 450°F (232°C) using direct heat with a cast iron grate installed. Place the chicken skewers on the grate, close the lid, and cook for 3 minutes per side. Transfer to a serving dish and squeeze lime juice over top before serving.

Grilled Italian Sausage & Orzo Soup

Servings:4

Cooking Time: 35 Minutes

Ingredients:

- 2 Italian sausages (Shannon uses Beyond Meat hot Italian sausages)
- 1 bell pepper (Shannon uses half yellow and half red), quartered, membrane and seeds removed
- 1 small to medium onion, peeled and quartered
- 1 15-oz can diced tomatoes with Italian seasoning
- 3 cups vegetable broth
- 1 medium zucchini, diced or two big handfuls of spinach
- ½ cup orzo, uncooked
- 1 tbsp Italian seasoning
- 3 cloves of garlic, minced
- Salt and pepper to taste
- Suggested toppings: fresh grated parmesan cheese and/or pearl mozzarella balls

Directions:

1. Preheat the grill to 375°F using direct heat with a cast iron grate installed.

2. Add the sausages, onions and peppers to the grid and grill until softening and charred. Dice into bite size pieces.

3. Lower the temperature of the kamado grill to 325°F with the dutch oven in the kamado grill to preheat.

4. Add all of the ingredients into the dutch oven and simmer for about 35 minutes or until the orzo is cooked, stirring every 10-12 minutes. Add more water as needed or to make the soup thinner if desired.

5. Serve with fresh grated parmesan cheese and/or pearl mozzarella balls.

Ancho Chili Grilled Kurobuta Pork With Bourbon Caramelized Apples

Servings:8

Cooking Time: 20 Minutes

Ingredients:

- 1 lb Kurobuta Frenched Pork Chops
- 1 Tbsp Dry Rub
- 2 Tbsp butter
- 2 shallots, thinly sliced
- 3 cloves of garlic, minced
- 2 Gala apples, cored and thinly sliced
- 2 tsp thyme leaves
- ½ tsp Kosher salt
- ¼ tsp black pepper, ground
- ½ cup bourbon
- 2 tsp Kosher salt
- 1 tsp Ancho chili powder
- ½ tsp black pepper, ground
- ¾ tsp coriander seeds, ground
- ¼ tsp cinnamon, ground
- ¼ tsp nutmeg, ground

Directions:

1. Preheat the grill to 550°F using direct heat with a cast iron grate installed.

2. Mix the dry rub ingredients together in a mixing bowl. Coat both sides of the Snake River Farms Kurobuta pork chops with the dry rub. Sear all four sides of the pork chops over direct flames for 30 seconds per side. Remove chops from the grill and set aside.

3. Place a cast iron skillet on the grill grate. Let the skillet preheat for 5-10 minutes, or until it has heated enough to sauté. Melt the butter in the cast iron pan and sauté the shallots and the garlic until soft. Add the apple, thyme leaves, salt, and pepper. Sauté until the apples start to brown and soften. Remove pan from the grill and deglaze with the bourbon.

4. Place the pork chops on the bed of apples and close the grill lid. Cook the chops until they reach an internal temperature of 140°F. Remove the cast iron skillet from the grill and let the pork chops rest for 10 minutes.

5. Slice the pork chops and serve with the bourbon caramelized apples.

Reuben Riffel's Yellow Bellied Pork

Servings:4

Cooking Time: 130 Minutes

Ingredients:

- 1⁄2 pork belly, deboned, fat scored finely
- 3 tbsp (45 ml) coarse salt
- 4 sprigs fresh thyme
- 1 1⁄2 cups (360 ml) curry sauce
- 8 dried apricots
- 1 cup (240 ml) water
- 1 cup (240 ml) sugar
- 2 star anise
- 2 tsp (10 ml) ground cinnamon
- 1 tbsp (15 ml) vegetable oil
- 2 medium onions, chopped
- 1⁄2 cup (120 ml) white wine vinegar
- 1 tsp (5 ml) garlic, chopped
- 1 tsp (5 ml) ginger, chopped
- 2 tbsp (30 ml) curry powder
- 2 tbsp (30 ml) garam masala
- 1 tbsp (15 ml) turmeric
- 1 tbsp (15 ml) paprika
- 3 allspice/pimentos
- 2 bay leaves
- 1 cup (240 ml) whole peeled tomatoes
- 1 cup (240 ml) water
- 1 cup (240 ml) chicken stock

- 1⁄2 cup (120 ml) sugar
- 1 tsp (5 ml) salt
- 1 tsp (5 ml) ground black pepper

Directions:

1. Rub the pork belly evenly with salt, focusing on the fatty part. Rub in the thyme evenly. Let cure for 30 minutes.

2. Preheat the grill to 325°F using direct heat with a cast iron grate installed. Place a drip pan on the platesetter and then add the stainless steel grid.

3. Dust the excess salt off the pork belly and add to the cooking grid, fatty side up. Cook for one hour and 40 minutes; flipping the meat over halfway through. Remove from the heat and let rest for 10 minutes before slicing. Serve drizzled with warm curry sauce and poached apricots.

4. Bring all the ingredients except the apricots to a boil. Turn down to a simmer, add the apricots and poach for two to three minutes. Remove from the heat and strain.

5. Set the kamado grill for direct cooking (without the platesetter) at 350°F.

6. Add the oil to a Stir-Fry & Paella Pan and cook the onions and spices until soft and fragrant. Deglaze the onion mixture with white wine vinegar and reduce the kamado grill temperature to 300°F.

7. Add the rest of the ingredients and cook for 20 to 30 minutes, or until the sauce has thickened to a thick gravy consistency. Blend until smooth and strain.

The Perfect Gift For Your Favorite Egghead

Servings:4
Cooking Time: 75 Minutes

Ingredients:

- 2 slabs St. Louis–style pork spareribs, about 4 pounds total
- 1⁄4 cup apple juice
- 1⁄4 cup cider vinegar
- 1⁄4 cup paprika
- 3 tablespoons raw sugar
- 2 tablespoons kosher salt
- 1 tablespoon granulated onion
- 1 tablespoon granulated garlic
- 1 teaspoon dried basil leaves
- 1 teaspoon cayenne pepper

Directions:

1. Preheat the grill to 300°F using direct heat with a cast iron grate installed. To make the rub, combine all of the ingredients in a small bowl and mix well. Peel the membrane off the back of each slab of ribs. Season the ribs on both sides using about half of the rub. Let the ribs rest for 15 minutes, or until the rub is tacky.

2. Lay the ribs, meaty side up, on the kamado grill cooking grid and cook for 2 hours. Flip the ribs and cook for 1 hour longer, or until the ribs are nicely browned on both sides.

3. Lay 2 big doubled sheets of heavy-duty aluminum foil on a work surface. Lay a rib slab, meaty side up, on the center of each doubled foil stack. In a small bowl, stir together the apple juice and vinegar, mixing well. Fold up the edges of each foil stack and then add 1⁄4 cup of the juice mixture to each packet. Close up each rib packet snugly, being careful not to puncture the foil with a rib bone. Reserve the remaining 1⁄2 cup juice mixture.

4. Put the ribs back in the kamado grill and cook for 1 hour, or until tender when poked with a toothpick or fork. Remove the ribs from the foil packets and place them, bone side down, on the

grid. Drizzle the ribs with 1/3 cup of the reserved juice mixture and sprinkle them with some of the remaining rub. Cook for about another 15 minutes, or until the ribs are dry.

5. Transfer to a platter and drizzle with the remaining juice mixture. With a big knife, cut the ribs into individual bones. Serve with any remaining rub on the side.

Tacos Al Pastor

Servings: 8
Cooking Time: 270 Minutes

Ingredients:
- 4lb (1.8kg) pork roast, thinly sliced at the butcher
- 1 small pineapple, peeled, cored, and cut lengthwise into quarters
- for the sauce
- 4 tsp vegetable oil
- 4 tbsp ancho chile powder
- 4 tbsp pasilla chile powder
- 2 tsp Mexican oregano
- 2 tsp ground cumin
- 2 tbsp achiote powder or paste
- 1/2 cup white vinegar
- 5 tsp kosher salt
- 4 tsp sugar
- 2 chipotle peppers in adobo
- 6 garlic cloves, peeled
- to serve
- 32 x 6-in (15.25-cm) corn tortillas, heated and kept warm
- 1 medium white onion, finely diced
- 1 bunch of fresh cilantro, roughly chopped
- 1 cup jarred salsa
- 3 limes, cut into wedges
- to smoke
- peach, apple, or pecan wood chunks

Directions:

1. Preheat the grill to 275°F (135°C). Once hot, add the wood chunks and install the heat deflector and a standard grate.

2. To make the sauce, on the stovetop in a saucepan over medium-high heat, heat oil until shimmering. Add ancho chile powder, pasilla chile powder, oregano, cumin, and achiote powder, and cook for 2 minutes. Add vinegar, salt, sugar, and chipotle peppers, and cook for 30 more seconds. Transfer the mixture to a blender and add the garlic. Blend on high speed until completely smooth, about 1 minute. Transfer sauce to a large bowl.

3. Add pork to the sauce, and toss until each piece is well coated. In a disposable aluminum baking dish, pile pork slices in a single layer, forming a tower. (The pork tower will extend beyond the rim of the pan.) Place the pan on the grate, close the lid, and cook until the meat is cooked through and completely tender, about 4 hours. (Pork will drip a lot.) Remove the pan from the grill and allow to cool slightly. Cover with aluminum foil and refrigerate for at least 2 hours or overnight.

4. Preheat the grill to 350°F (177°C) using indirect heat with a standard grate installed and a cast iron skillet on the grate. Remove pork from the fridge and scrape off the solidified fat. Slice vertically through the pork tower, creating fine shavings of meat.

5. Add the shaved pork to the hot skillet along with the pineapple quarters. Close the grill lid and cook until the meat is hot and tender and pineapple begins to soften, about 30 minutes, stirring occasionally.

6. Remove pork and pineapple from the grill. Serve wrapped in double-stacked corn tortillas and topped with onion, cilantro, salsa, and a squeeze of lime.

Pork Belly Burnt Ends

Servings:2

Cooking Time: 180 Minutes

Ingredients:

- 1 pound piece of pork belly
- Your favorite barbecue rub
- Your favorite barbecue sauce
- Honey
- Apple juice

Directions:

1. Preheat the grill to 275°F using direct heat with a cast iron grate installed.

2. Trim the pork belly and cut the pork belly into 1" cubes. Cover the pork belly pieces in your favorite BBQ rub. Place pork belly pieces on the cooking grid and smoke for 3 hours, spraying with apple juice every hour until the pork reaches and internal temperature of 190°F.

3. Remove the pork pieces from the kamado grill and place them in an aluminum pan. Toss the pork belly pieces with BBQ sauce until evenly covered. Drizzle with honey and put the aluminum pan back on the grill. Cook the pork belly and cook for another hour until the sauce has reduced and caramelized.

Croque Monsieur & Croque Madam

Servings:6

Cooking Time: 30 Minutes

Ingredients:

- 4 slices smoked ham
- 4 slices sourdough bread
- 4 slices smoked provolone
- 1 cup shredded gruyere
- 2 tbsp butter
- 1 egg (for croque madam)
- 2 tbsp olive oil
- 1 cup béchamel sauce
- 1 tbsp butter
- 1 tbsp flour
- 3/4 cup warmed milk
- ¼ cup warmed heavy cream (added to milk to warm)
- 1 tsp salt (and salt to taste)
- 1 tsp course black pepper
- 2 tsp ground nutmeg

Directions:

1. Preheat the grill to 400°F using direct heat with a cast iron grate installed. Add the plancha griddle on half of the spander, with the half-moon baking stone, grid and a cast iron skillet on the other half.

2. To build the sandwiches, spread a layer of béchamel sauce on 2 slices of bread, then top with ham, provolone cheese, and the gruyere cheese; 2 slices for each piece of bread. Spread béchamel sauce on the last 2 slices of bread and place them on top of the sandwiches. On the top pieces of bread, spread more béchamel sauce and the remaining gruyere cheese on top.

3. Coat the plancha with olive oil and add both sandwiches. Cook until the bottom of the sandwich is golden brown and the provolone cheese is melted. Using your igniter, toast the top of the sandwich until it looks as if it has been broiled. Remove both sandwiches and set aside.

4. Melt butter on the plancha and fry your egg over easy or over medium. Top one sandwich with the egg; this is a Croque Madam, the sandwich without is a Croque Monsieur. Cut in half, and serve!

5. For the béchamel sauce, melt the butter in the cast iron skillet and add flour. Cook until the mixture turns golden brown and is fragrant.

Slowly add the milk and cream while whisking the mixture to ensure there are no lumps. Once the milk and cream are completely mixed in removed the skillet from the heat and continue to whisk until the mixture has a creamy texture and is thick enough to cover the back of a spoon. If the mixture gets too thick, slowly mix in more milk until desired consistency. Add salt, pepper and nutmeg then set aside.

Sriracha Pork Chops

Servings:4
Cooking Time: 9 Minutes

Ingredients:
- 4 (1") boneless pork chops
- 2 Tablespoons Better Than Bouillon Reduced Sodium Roasted Chicken Base
- 1 Tablespoon minced garlic
- 1 Tablespoon Sriracha sauce
- 1 Tablespoon freshly chopped cilantro
- 1 Tablespoon freshly squeezed lime juice
- 1/4 cup brown sugar
- 2 teaspoons freshly minced ginger

Directions:
1. Instructions Mix the Roasted Chicken Base, garlic, sriracha, cilantro, lime juice, brown sugar and ginger in a small mixing bowl. Add half of the mixture to a resealable plastic bag and add the pork chops and refrigerate for at least 3 hours and up to 8 hours.
2. Reserve the rest of the marinade, covered and refrigerated until ready to use.
3. Preheat the grill to 425°F using direct heat with a cast iron grate installed.
4. Remove the pork chops from the marinade and place directly onto the grill. Grill for 4 minutes. Using tongs, turn the pork chops and brush with the reserved marinade. Grill for an additional 4 – 5 minutes.
5. Remove the pork chops from the kamado grill and brush with the reserved marinade before serving.
6. Serve immediately.

Braised Beer Brats And Sauerkraut

Servings:8
Cooking Time: 20 Minutes

Ingredients:
- 4 bratwursts
- 12 oz sauerkraut
- 1 bottle of beer
- 4 buns
- German-style mustard

Directions:
1. Preheat the grill to 400°F using direct heat with a cast iron grate installed.
2. Put bratwurst into the cast iron skillet, pour beer over the top and add the sauerkraut to the pan. Braise for 15 to 20 minutes, or until the liquid has reduced by half.
3. Remove the bratwurst from the skillet and grill over direct heat until grill marks have appeared. Toast the buns on the grill.
4. Once the bratwursts have the desired grill marks put them back into the skillet. Remove buns and the cast iron from the grill. Smear mustard on each side of the bun and add brats, top with sauerkraut. Enjoy!

Honey Pecan Chorizo Jalapeño Poppers

Servings:6
Cooking Time: 15 Minutes

Ingredients:

- 16 jalapeños (not too large so the bacon wraps around nicely)
- 1 package standard cut bacon
- ½ package pork chorizo
- 1 16 oz block of cream cheese
- Deez Nuts Pecan Rub (substitute Honey Hog or Honey Hog Hot)

Directions:

1. Preheat the grill to 275°F using direct heat with a cast iron grate installed.

2. We recommend oak, hickory or pecan wood for this smoke. There is something cool about pecan on pecan action thought! Heat a skillet over medium heat. Fry the chorizo until it is fully cooked. Drain the fat off when the chorizo is done. Immediately mix the chorizo and cream cheese together in a small bowl. The warm chorizo will help soften the cream cheese. Add Deez Nuts Honey Pecan rub to taste and mix well. A heavy dose is recommended. You aren't going to hurt it. Cut the stem off and core each jalapeño. Remove all seeds. Leave the membranes in if you want the heat! Cut the jalapeños in half and fill each jalapeño up with cream cheese mixture. Wrap each jalapeño with a 1/2 slice of bacon. Dust the tops of the jalapeño poppers with more Deez Nuts Pecan Rub. Smoke the peppers for an hour or until the bacon looks perfect! Allow to cool 10 – 15 minutes and then enjoy one of our favorite appetizers!

Breakfast Fatty

Servings:8
Cooking Time: 90 Minutes

Ingredients:

- 1 package of bacon
- 1 package of breakfast sausage
- 5 large eggs
- 1 cup of shredded cheese (3 cheese blend works well)
- ½ white onion, chopped
- ½ green bell pepper, chopped
- Meat Church Honey Hog BBQ Rub
- Salt & pepper

Directions:

1. Preheat the grill to 275°F using direct heat with a cast iron grate installed.

2. Start by lightly sautéing the onions and bell peppers on the Half Moon Plancha Griddle. Scramble the eggs and add the onion and bell pepper mixture. Salt and pepper to taste and set aside.

3. Next make a 6×6 bacon weave. Lay 6 pieces of bacon side by side (touching) on parchment paper, which will help to prevent sticking. Then weave the remaining 6 pieces of bacon across those 6. Make sure your bacon weave is tight.

4. Next layer the breakfast sausage evenly across your bacon weave. Make sure the sausage extends to the edges of the bacon weave.

5. Add the scrambled egg mixture evenly across the sausage. Then spread the shredded cheese evenly across the top of the eggs. Top with a sprinkling of Honey Hog BBQ rub.

6. Carefully roll the bacon weave up tightly to form what looks like a burrito. Tuck the ends of the bacon into the side of the breakfast fatty to secure all the contents.

7.   Cover all sides with a nice coat of Honey Hog BBQ rub.

8.   Place the breakfast fatty on the grid and cook until the internal temperature reaches at least 160°F. That will ensure the ground sausage is fully cooked. This will take about 1 ½ hours.

9.   Remove the breakfast fatty from the cooker and let rest for at least 10 minutes. Slice 1" thick slices. This is great by itself, on a biscuit or as Matt does in Texas, on a fresh flour tortilla!

Stir-fried Cucumber And Pork With Golden Garlic

Servings:2
Cooking Time: 5 Minutes

Ingredients:

- ½ cup (120 ml) peanut or vegetable oil
- 3 tbsp (45 ml) chopped garlic
- 12 ounces (340 g) lean pork shoulder or butt, cut into 1⁄4 inch (65 cm) thick bite-sized slices
- 1 ½ tsp (8 ml) cornstarch
- 3 tsp (15 ml) soy sauce
- 1⁄4 tsp (1.5 ml) sugar
- 3⁄4 tsp (3.75 ml) salt
- 8 slices ginger, smashed
- 1 large English cucumber, ends trimmed, halved lengthwise and cut on the diagonal into 1⁄4 inch (65 cm) thick slices

Directions:

1.   Preheat the grill to 600°F using direct heat with a cast iron grate installed. Once the kamado grill is steadily at this temperature, shut the bottom draft door and carefully open the lid.

2.   Carbon Steel Wok, heat the pan until a bead of water vaporizes within 1 to 2 seconds of contact. Carefully add the oil and garlic and cook, stirring 30 seconds to 1 minute or until the garlic is light golden.

3.   Remove the pan from the heat. Remove the garlic with a metal skimmer and put on a plate lined with paper towels. Carefully remove the oil from the woke and reserve. Wash the pan and dry it thoroughly.

4.   In a shallow bowl combine the pork, cornstarch, 11⁄2 teaspoon (8 ml) of the soy sauce, sugar and 1⁄4 teaspoon (1.5 ml) of the salt. Ina small bowl combine the remaining 11⁄2 teaspoon (8 ml) soy sauce and 1 tablespoon (15 ml) cold water.

5.   Again, heat the wok over high heat until a beat of water vaporizes within 1 to 2 seconds of contact. Swirl in 2 tablespoons (30 ml) of the reserved garlic oil, add the ginger slices; then, using a spatula, stir-fry 30 seconds or until the ginger is fragrant. Push the ginger to the sides of the wok, carefully add the pork, and spread it evenly in one layer in the pan.

6.   Cook undisturbed 1 minute, letting the pork begin to sear. Then stir-fry 1 minute or until the pork is lightly browned but now cooked through. Add the cucumber and stir-fry 30 seconds or until well combined. Sprinkle on the remaining 1⁄2 tsp (2.5 ml) salt, swirl the reserved soy sauce mixture into the pan and stir-fry 1 minute or until the pork is just cooked and the cucumber begins to wilt. Stir in the reserved garlic.

Dill Pickle Injected Chicken Bog

Servings:4
Cooking Time: 40 Minutes

Ingredients:
- 2 boneless, skinless chicken breasts
- Dill Pickle Hot sauce
- 4 cheddarwurst sausages

- 4 stalks celery, chopped
- ½ onion, minced
- 4 cloves of garlic, minced
- 1 qt. water
- 1 chicken bouillon cube
- 2 cups white rice
- Salt and pepper to taste

Directions:

1. Preheat the grill to 400°F using direct heat with a cast iron grate installed. Place the half-moon cast iron griddle with the flat side up on top of the grid and the dutch oven on the other half of the grid.

2. Season the chicken with salt and pepper, and inject with dill pickle hot sauce. Let the chicken marinate for 30 minutes.

3. Cook the chicken and sausages on the plancha until the chicken is cooked through and the sausages have some color, about 15-20 minutes.

4. While the chicken and sausages are cooking, add water, bouillon cube, garlic, onion, celery into the dutch oven. Remove the chicken and sausages, cube into bite size pieces, and add to the dutch oven. Add rice to the dutch oven and put the lid on. Cook for 20 minutes until rice is fully cooked, making sure to stir.

5. Remove from the grill, enjoy!

Twice-smoked Ham

Servings: 16
Cooking Time: 210 Minutes

Ingredients:

- 18lb (8kg) bone-in whole or spiral-cut smoked ham, at room temperature
- 1 cup water
- for the glaze
- 1 cup sugar
- 2 tbsp water
- 1 tbsp fennel seeds
- 1 tbsp coriander seeds
- 4 star anise pods
- 4 bay leaves
- 2 cinnamon sticks
- 2 garlic cloves
- 1-in (2.5-cm) piece fresh ginger, thinly sliced
- 1 dried red chile pepper
- 1 tsp finely grated orange zest
- 2 cups bourbon
- 2 tbsp low-sodium soy sauce
- 2 tbsp honey
- to smoke
- hickory or apple wood chunks

Directions:

1. Preheat the grill to 300°F (149°C) using indirect heat. Once hot, add the wood chunks and install the heat deflector and a standard grate. Place the precooked ham in a large roasting pan (a disposable aluminum pan works well) and add water. Place the pan on the grate, close the lid, and smoke until an instant-read thermometer inserted in the thickest part of the meat reads 120°F (49°C), about 2 hours and 45 minutes, basting occasionally with any accumulated juices.

2. To make the glaze, in a medium saucepan, combine sugar and water, and place the pan on the stovetop over medium-high heat. Cook until a light golden syrup forms, about 8 to 10 minutes, swirling the pan occasionally.

3. Remove from the heat and quickly add fennel seeds, coriander seeds, star anise, bay leaves, cinnamon, garlic, ginger, chile pepper, and orange zest. Let sit until fragrant, about 20 seconds. Carefully add the bourbon, soy sauce, and honey. Return the glaze to medium heat and

bring to a simmer until slightly thickened, about 10 minutes, stirring occasionally.

4. Once ham reaches 120°F (49°C), brush it with the glaze. Continue smoking until the top is lightly caramelized, about 30 minutes more, brushing with glaze every 10 minutes.

5. Transfer ham to a platter and let rest for 15 minutes. Skim the fat from the pan and transfer the juices to a bowl. Slice and serve with the warm pan juices.

Smoked Porchetta On The Grill

Servings:12
Cooking Time: 370 Minutes

Ingredients:
- 1 pork belly
- 1 cup kosher salt
- 4 star anis, ground
- 10 black peppercorns, ground
- 5 allspice, ground
- 10 white peppercorns, ground
- 10 garlic cloves, smashed
- 3 sprigs thyme, chopped
- ½ cup granulated sugar
- 3 bunches broccoli raab
- 7 garlic cloves, shaved thin
- 1 tbsp butter
- 3 tsp red pepper flakes
- 1 tbsp lemon juice
- Salt and pepper to taste

Directions:
1. Twenty-four hours before your cook, mix all the aromatics together and rub into the pork belly on both sides. Cure the pork belly in a cooler.

2. Preheat the grill to 250°F using direct heat with a cast iron grate installed.

3. Rinse off the cure, then tie the pork belly into a roll with butcher twine. Place the rolled and tied pork belly in the grill. Smoke the belly until tender, around 4-6 hours or until an internal temperature reaches 165°F. Remove from the grill, untie and let rest for 10 minutes.

4. While the pork belly is resting, set up the kamado grill for direct cooking without the platesetter at 400°F.

5. Place the garlic and butter in a cast iron skillet. Cook garlic until it starts to brown then add the broccoli and the remaining ingredients. Cook the broccoli until it starts to wilt, roughly 5 minutes. Tip: add a touch of water if needed to help keep the pan from getting too hot. Remove from kamado grill and serve.

6. Slice the belly to desired thickness and serve with the braised broccoli raab.

Brunswick Stew

Servings:8
Cooking Time: 120 Minutes

Ingredients:
- 2 lbs. precooked pulled pork
- 2 lbs. chicken breast
- 1 28 oz. can crushed tomatoes
- 32 oz. chicken broth
- 1 package frozen lima beans
- 1 lb. shoe peg corn
- 1/2 lb. red potatoes cut in half
- 1 tbsp garlic salt
- 2 garlic cloves, minced
- ½ yellow onion, diced
- 2 tsp kosher salt
- 1 tbsp olive oil
- ¼ cup Bold & Tangy Carolina Style BBQ sauce

Directions:
1. Preheat the grill to 300°F using direct heat with a cast iron grate installed.

2. In your dutch oven with olive oil, sear and cook the chicken breast, remove and cut into cubes and put back into the dutch oven.

3. Add all the other ingredients and mix. Cook for approximately two hours. Serve with cornbread, or biscuits.

Tony Chachere's Jambalaya

Servings:2
Cooking Time: 25 Minutes

Ingredients:
- 2 chicken breasts
- Sweet & Smoky Seasoning, to taste
- ¼ cup olive oil
- 4 smoked sausage links, cut into bite-sized pieces
- 2 bell peppers, chopped
- ½ red onion, chopped
- One box Tony Chachere's Creole Jambalaya Rice Dinner Mix
- 2¼ cups water

Directions:
1. Preheat the grill to 375°F using direct heat with a cast iron grate installed.

2. Season the chicken breasts with Sweet & Smoky Seasoning, cut into bite-sized pieces.

3. Place a dutch oven on the cooking grid to heat. Add the olive oil, then the next five ingredients. Cook for two minutes until slightly tender.

4. Add the water and bring to a boil; add the Jambalaya Rice Dinner Mix and stir all ingredients together. Cover and cook for appx. 25 minutes until most of the liquid is absorbed.

Glazed Pork Belly With Sweet Potato

Servings:6
Cooking Time: 90 Minutes

Ingredients:
- 1¾ lbs (800 g) pork belly
- Agave nectar for drizzling
- Sea salt flakes
- 12 small sprigs of thyme
- 1 cup (240 ml) peach jam
- ½ cup (120 ml) barbecue sauce
- 3 tbsp (45 ml) bourbon whiskey
- 3 tbsp (45 ml) agave nectar
- 3 tbsp (45 ml) flower honey
- 6 tbsp (90 ml) smoked paprika powder (pimentón dulce)
- 2 tbsp (30 ml) dried thyme
- 1 tbsp (15 ml) garlic powder
- 1 tbsp (15 ml) onion powder
- 1 tbsp (15 ml) freshly ground black pepper
- 2 tbsp (30 ml) muscovado sugar or brown caster sugar
- 1 tbsp (15 ml) ground ginger
- pinch of chilli powder
- 6 sweet potatoes
- 7 tsp (35 ml) ground cinnamon
- 1 ⅓ cups (300 g) butter + extra for greasing the pan

Directions:
1. Preheat the grill to 375°F using direct heat with a cast iron grate installed.

2. Remove most of the fat layer from the pork belly, allowing a layer of ⅛inch (3-4 mm) of the soft white fat to remain. Cut the layer of fat on the pork belly crosswise.

3. Lightly rub the pork belly with the rub, reserving about ⅓ of the rub, and drizzle with

agave nectar. Sprinkle with sea salt flakes and rub into the meat.

4. Sprinkle a handful Pecan Smoking Chips on the charcoal embers and add the platesetter for indirect cooking and Cast Iron Grid (flat side up). Lay the pork belly with the fat upwards on the grid and close the lid of the grill. Stabilize the temperature at 325°F and smoke the pork belly for 35-40 minutes.

5. With a basting brush, coat all sides of the pork belly with the glaze, reserving about of the glaze. Continue to cook until the internal temperature of the pork reaches 165°F. Remove from the kamado grill and loosely cover with foil. Raise the temperature of the kamado grill to 375°F.

6. Cut the pork belly into 1½inch (4 cm) cubes and lay them on the Cast Iron Plancha Griddle. Top with the remaining glaze and rub.

7. Place the Cast Iron Plancha Griddle with the pork on the grid. Grill for approximately 5 minutes until the glaze is caramelized and the pork is hot.

8. Put all ingredients for the glaze in a pan and bring to a boil on the stovetop while stirring often. Turn the heat to low and simmer gently for approximately 10 minutes.

9. Mix all ingredients for the rub together.

10. Wash and pat dry the sweet potatoes; cut into halves lengthwise. Grease a Cast Iron Skillet with butter and add the potatoes, cut edge upwards. Dust with 6 teaspoons of the cinnamon, cut 1 cup (225 g) of butter into thin slices and arrange the slices over the sweet potatoes.

11. Cover the skillet with foil and place in the grill; cook the potatoes for 45 minutes until the flesh is soft.

12. Scoop the cooked flesh of six potato halves and place in a bowl. Cut the remaining butter into cubes and add to the potatoes. Sprinkle with the remaining cinnamon and fold in gently. Scoop a sixth of the mixture onto each potato half. Garnish with the thyme and serve with the pork belly.

Cider-brined Pork Chops

Servings:4
Cooking Time: 8 Minutes

Ingredients:

- 2 cups apple cider
- 1 cup water
- 1⁄4 cup salt
- 1⁄4 cup sugar
- 2 tablespoons whole-grain mustard
- 3 sprigs fresh rosemary
- 10 black peppercorns
- 1 bay leaf
- 4 (14-ounce) center cut pork loin chops

Directions:

1. To make brine, place first 8 ingredients in saucepan and bring to boil; let cool to room temperature. Refrigerate until chilled, about 1 hour.

2. Pour brine into 1-gallon zip-close plastic bag and add pork chops. Seal tightly and refrigerate for 12 to 24 hours.

3. Remove pork chops, discarding brine, and pat dry.

4. Preheat the grill to 400°F using direct heat with a cast iron grate installed.

5. Cook pork chops on kamado grill for about 8 minutes per side or until cooked through to center. Serve with Cider Bourbon BBQ Sauce. Try with Cabot Habanero Cheddar Hush Puppies.

Ham Muffinini

Servings:4

Cooking Time: 7 Minutes

Ingredients:

- 4 Nature's Own 100% Whole Wheat English Muffins, split
- 8 very thin asparagus spears
- 8 slices Swiss or Gruyere cheese
- ¼ pound sliced smoked ham
- Olive oil
- Salt
- Pepper
- Dijon mustard

Directions:

1. Preheat the grill to 400°F using direct heat with a cast iron grate installed.

2. Brush asparagus spears lightly with oil; season with salt and pepper. Place on the griddle; cook 3 minutes or until lightly charred. Cool slightly; cut each spear crosswise in half.

3. Meanwhile spread mustard over muffin halves. Layer each of 4 muffin halves with 1 slice cheese. Top evenly with ham, asparagus, remaining cheese and muffin halves; press sandwiches together slightly. Brush outside of sandwiches lightly with oil.

4. Cook sandwiches on the griddle 3 to 4 minutes or until browned and cheese melts.

Pulled Pork Nachos With Fire-roasted Salsa

Servings:6

Cooking Time: 7 Minutes

Ingredients:

- 1 lb. pulled pork
- 1 bag tortilla chips
- 1 can black beans, strained
- 2 cups shredded cheddar cheese
- 1 cup guacamole
- 1 cup sour cream
- ½ cup pickled jalapenos
- ¼ cup minced cilantro
- 1 cup cheese dip
- 6 tomatoes
- 4 jalapeño peppers
- 8 cloves garlic
- 1 red onion
- 3 scallions
- ¼ cup chopped cilantro
- 2 tbsp lime juice
- ½ tbsp black pepper
- 2 tbsp kosher salt
- 1 tbsp Ancho Chile & Coffee Seasoning
- 1 tbsp chili powder
- 1 tbsp cumin

Directions:

1. Preheat the grill to 400°F using direct heat with a cast iron grate installed.

2. Add the tortilla chips to the cast iron skillet and top with pulled pork, beans, cheese and pickled jalapenos. Place on the kamado grill for 5-7 minutes or until the shredded cheese has melted. While the nachos are on the grill, add cheese dip to the saucepot and place in the kamado grill to heat.

3. Remove nachos and cheese dip from the grill. Pour the cheese dip all over the nachos, top with guacamole, sour cream and fire-roasted salsa. Garnish with cilantro. Enjoy!

4. Place the whole tomatoes, jalapenos, onion, and scallions directly on the grid and grill until there are char marks. Remove from the kamado grill and cut all of the vegetables into smaller pieces and put in the blender. If a milder salsa is desired remove the seeds from the jalapeno

peppers. Add the garlic, lime juice, cilantro, pepper, salt, Ancho Chili & Coffee Seasoning, chili powder and cumin to the blender. Blend until desired texture. Add more salt to taste.

Beer-infused Baby Back Ribs

Servings: 2
Cooking Time: 300 Minutes

Ingredients:
- 1 rack of baby back ribs, about 3lb (1.4kg) in total
- BBQ sauce, to serve
- for the brine
- 3/4 cup kosher salt
- 1/3 cup packed light brown sugar
- 1/3 cup raw sugar
- 1 1/2 tsp pink curing salt
- 3 cups hot water
- 2 cups beer, preferably brown ale or lager
- 2 tbsp pickling spice
- to smoke
- apple or apricot wood chunks

Directions:
1. To make the brine, in a large bowl, whisk together kosher salt, brown sugar, raw sugar, pink curing salt, and hot water until sugars and salts dissolve. Whisk in beer and pickling spice, and set aside to cool to room temperature.
2. Place ribs on a cutting board and remove the thin, papery membrane from the back of the ribs. Cut the rack in half widthwise between the middle bones. Place ribs in a heavy-duty resealable plastic bag and add brine to cover. Squeeze out any excess air and place in an aluminum pan or a roasting pan. (Any extra brine can be refrigerated and saved for a later use.) Refrigerate for 24 hours.
3. Remove ribs from the brine and pat dry with paper towels. Arrange ribs on a wire rack over a rimmed baking sheet and let dry uncovered in the fridge for 2 hours.
4. Preheat the grill to 225°F (107°C). Once hot, add the wood chunks and install the heat deflector and a standard grate. Place ribs bone side down on the grate, close the lid, and smoke until the meat shrinks back from the ends of the bones by 1/2 inch (1.25cm), about 4 to 5 hours. Transfer ribs to a cutting board and cut into individual ribs.
5. Place ribs on a serving platter, brush with BBQ sauce, and serve immediately. (For more charring and caramelization, return the sauce-coated ribs to the grill for 5 to 10 minutes more before serving.)

Cedar Plank Pork Tenderloin

Servings: 8
Cooking Time: 20 Minutes

Ingredients:
- 2 pork tenderloins
- 1 cup Basic Steak Marinade (not just for steaks!)
- 2 cedar planks (Be sure they are untreated cedar)

Directions:
1. Place the pork tenderloins and Basic Steak Marinade in a zip top bag for 30 minutes.
2. Grilling:
3. Preheat the grill to 425°F using direct heat with a cast iron grate installed.
4. Place the cedar planks directly on the grid and close the dome for 3 minutes.
5. Turn the planks and place the tenderloins directly on the heated planks.
6. Close the dome for 10 minutes.

7. Turn the tenderloins once and close the dome for another 5-10 minutes or until the internal temperature reaches 155°F.

8. Remove the tenderloins and allow them to rest for 5 minutes before slicing.

Spatchcocked Chicken

Servings: 4
Cooking Time: 50 Minutes

Ingredients:

- 1 whole young chicken, about 4lb (1.8kg) in total, skin on
- kosher salt and freshly ground black pepper
- for the brine
- 1/2 cup kosher salt
- 1/2 cup packed light brown sugar
- 3 tbsp pickling spice
- 6 cups hot water
- for the tomato relish
- 2 tbsp extra virgin olive oil
- 1 tbsp red wine vinegar
- 14.5oz (411g) can diced tomatoes, drained
- 2 garlic cloves, minced
- 2 tsp kosher salt
- 5 basil leaves, chopped
- 10 Kalamata olives, pitted and chopped
- 1 small red onion, diced
- 2oz (55g) dry feta cheese, diced

Directions:

1. To make the brine, in a large bowl, whisk together salt, brown sugar, pickling spice, and water until salt and sugar have dissolved. Add ice cubes a few at a time until the liquid is no longer hot. Place chicken in a large resealable plastic bag and add brine to fully cover. (Any extra brine can be refrigerated and saved for a later use.) Refrigerate for 6 to12 hours.

2. Remove chicken from the brine and pat dry with paper towels. Place the bird breast side down on a cutting board. Using poultry shears, cut along one side of the backbone, starting at the thigh meat and cutting away from you. Rotate chicken and cut down the opposite side of the backbone. Remove and discard the backbone. Turn chicken breast side up, press firmly on the breastbone to flatten, and tuck the wings behind the back. Rub the skin with salt and pepper to taste.

3. Preheat the grill to 375°F (191°C) using indirect heat with a cast iron grate installed. Place the chicken skin side down on the grate, close the lid, and roast until the internal temperature of the thigh meat reaches 170°F (77°C), about 50 minutes, turning once.

4. To make the tomato relish, in a large bowl, stir together oil, vinegar, tomatoes, garlic, salt, basil, olives, and onion. Gently stir in feta.

5. Transfer the chicken to a platter and let rest for 10 minutes before serving with the tomato relish.

Braised Carnitas With Chimichurri Sauce

Servings:8
Cooking Time: 300 Minutes

Ingredients:

- 4 lbs. boneless pork shoulder
- 3 tbsp olive oil
- 1 can of Coca-Cola
- 2 oranges, juiced
- 6 limes, 2 juiced and 4 sliced in wedges for serving
- 2 jalapeños, seeded and chopped
- 1 yellow onion, diced
- 2 tbsp garlic, minced

- Flour tortillas
- 2 tbsp oregano
- 3 tsp cumin
- 3 tbsp olive oil
- 3 tbsp salt
- 3 tbsp pepper
- 3 tsp. minced garlic
- ½ tbsp. salt (more to taste if needed)
- 2 cups cilantro, finely chopped
- 3 tbsp oregano
- 1 cup parsley, finely chopped
- ¼ cup minced red onion
- 1 lime, juiced
- 2 tbsp. white wine vinegar
- 1 cup EVOO

Directions:

1. Preheat the grill to 400°F using direct heat with a cast iron grate installed.

2. Rinse pork and pat dry. Season the entire pork shoulder liberally with the rub.

3. Place a dutch oven on the grid and add the oil to heat. Add the pork shoulder and sear on all sides until lightly browned.

4. Remove the dutch oven from the grill. Add the platesetter for indirect cooking and stabilize the kamado grill at 300°F.

5. Arrange the shoulder in the dutch oven with the fat cap facing up. Pour the Coca-Cola, orange juice and lime juice into the dutch oven. Add the jalapeños, onion and garlic over the top of the pork. Cook for 4 ½ to 5 hours until meat pulls apart easily.

6. Mix all the ingredients together.

7. Crush the garlic and salt together to make a paste. Add cilantro, oregano, parsley, red onion and lime juice until combined. Add white wine vinegar and EVOO, mix and add salt/pepper to taste. Serve over the carnitas with tortillas.

Mona Lisa's Glazed Smoked Ham

Servings:4
Cooking Time: 270 Minutes

Ingredients:

- 1 Ham 10-12 lbs
- 1-20 oz. can round sliced pineapple
- 1 jar maraschino cherries
- 2 boxes brown sugar

Directions:

1. Preheat the grill to 350°F using direct heat with a cast iron grate installed..

2. Rinse ham with cold water, pat dry, and set aside.

3. Take the juice from the pineapple and mix well with the brown sugar to make a nice thick syrupy glaze. Next add the pineapple to the ham putting a cherry in the hole of each pineapple round. Finally pour the glaze over the ham.

4. Loosely cover the ham with aluminum foil and cook for 3-4 hours basting the ham with the pan juice every 30 min.

5. Let stand for 30 min. Slice and serve.

Pig Candy

Servings:6
Cooking Time: 20 Minutes

Ingredients:

- 1 cup brown sugar
- 1/2 tsp cayenne pepper
- 1 lb thick cut bacon
- 1/2 cup maple syrup

Directions:

1. Preheat the grill to 350°F using direct heat with a cast iron grate installed. Cover a baking sheet in foil, and place a wire rack on the baking

sheet, or use a Half Moon Perforated Cooking Grid.

2. Mix together brown sugar and cayenne pepper in a small bowl. Cover strips of bacon with brown sugar mixture. Then, place the bacon on the wire rack or cooking grid.

3. Place baking sheet in the kamado grill and allow to cook until the bacon starts to crisp. Then brush the top of the bacon with maple syrup, flip the bacon and brush the other side with maple syrup as well. Allow to continue to cook until it is to your preference of doneness. Remove and serve.

4. You may serve it with a small side of additional maple syrup for dipping if you'd like it to be extra sweet!

Perfect Ribs

Servings:6
Cooking Time: 45 Minutes

Ingredients:

- 4 tbsp (60 ml) paprika
- 2 tbsp (30 ml) oregano
- 1 tbsp (15 ml) garlic powder
- 1 tbsp (15 ml) brown sugar
- 1 tbsp (15 ml) onion powder
- 1 tbsp (15 ml) dry mustard
- 2 tbsp (30 ml) cumin
- 2 tbsp (30 ml) salt

Directions:

1. Preheat the grill to 300°F using direct heat with a cast iron grate installed.

2. Combine all spices in a small bowl. Remove the membrane from the ribs and apply seasoning to both sides.

3. Place the ribs in the Rib and Roast Rack, bone side down, and cook for one hour. Flip the ribs and rotate the rack 180°. Cook for another hour.

4. Baste the ribs with the preserves (we used salted caramel peach preserves) then wrap tightly in foil – you do not want any gaps in the wrap or you will steam the ribs. Cook for an additional 30 minutes, then unwrap the ribs and place directly on the grid for a final 15 minutes to allow the glaze to tighten up.

5. Let rest for 5 to 10 minutes before serving.

Leg Of Warthog

Servings:8
Cooking Time: 240 Minutes

Ingredients:

- 1 Leg of warthog (if warthog is unavailable, substitute pork loin or wild boar)
- 1 lb. (450 g) streaky bacon
- 2 tsp (10 ml) mixture of garlic and herb seasonings
- 1 tsp (5 ml) ground cloves
- 1 cup (250 ml) vegetable stock powder
- 2 tsp (10 ml) ground ginger
- Healthy splash of white wine
- 1 cup (250 ml) apricot jam
- Zest of 1 naartjie (or tangerine)
- ½ cup (125 ml) olive oil
- Salt and black pepper to taste
- 4 cups (1 liter) water
- 1 lemon
- 1 large carrot, chopped
- 1 celery stick, chopped
- 4 whole chili peppers

Directions:

1. Roll the bacon in the garlic and herb seasonings. Lard the warthog leg first with a piece of naartjie peel and then with the seasoned bacon. Keep bacon in place with toothpicks.

2.   Mix the remainder of the dry ingredients and wet ingredients together to make the marinade. Experiment and add whatever you like from the cupboard. The marinade needs to be sweet and sticky. In South Africa, this is called "sommer gooi" cooking ("just throw").

3.   Place the leg in a Dutch Oven, add marinade and cover. Marinate for 24 hours in the refrigerator.

4.   Preheat the grill to 300°F using direct heat with a cast iron grate installed.

5.   Add extra water, carrots, quartered lemon, celery and chili peppers to the Dutch Oven.

6.   Cover and cook slowly for about 4 hours. Baste the leg from time to time and check to make sure leg is still sitting in at least 1 to 2 inches (2.5 to 5 cm) of liquid.

7.   Remove leg from Dutch Oven, place on the cooking grid and cook for another hour, basting regularly. When done, the meat should be easily coming off the bone and should fall apart.

8.   Allow to rest for 10 minutes before serving.

9.   While the meat is resting, use the leftover juices in the Dutch Oven to make gravy. The gravy should be sweet with a slight chili bite. Add extra apricot jam and chilis if necessary.

10. Serve with chili steamed cabbage and garlic mashed potatoes.

Maple Brined Pork Chops

Servings:4

Cooking Time: 14 Minutes

Ingredients:

- 4 bone-in pork chops, about 3⁄4 in (2 cm) thick
- 1 recipe cold Maple Brine
- 2 tbsp pure maple syrup
- 2 cups (480 ml) water, plus 2 cups (480 ml) ice water
- 1⁄2 cup (120 ml) pure maple syrup
- 1⁄4 cup (60 g) Morton's Kosher Salt
- 1 tbsp vanilla extract
- 1 tsp granulated onion
- 1 tsp black pepper
- 1⁄2 tsp cinnamon
- 1⁄4 tsp ground nutmeg

Directions:

1.   Place the chops in a large heavy-duty zip-top bag. Pour the brine over them. Seal the bag, squeezing out as much air as possible. Place the bag in a pan or bowl in case of leakage and refrigerate it for 3 to 4 hours, occasionally moving the chops around within the bag.

2.   Preheat the grill to 350°F using direct heat with a cast iron grate installed.

3.   Remove the chops from the brine and rinse them under cold water. Dry the chops well. Place them on the kamado grill and cook them for 5 to 6 minutes, until they're golden brown. Flip them over and cook them for another 5 to 6 minutes, until they reach an internal temperature of 150°F deep in the center. Remove them to a plate and brush each chop with the maple syrup on all sides. Serve one chop to each guest.

4.   In a medium saucepan over medium heat, combine the 2 cups (480 ml) water, maple syrup, salt, vanilla, granulated onion, pepper, cinnamon, and nutmeg. Mix them well. Bring the mixture to a simmer, stirring often. Cook it for 1 to 2 minutes, until the salt and syrup are dissolved. Add the ice water to a large bowl. Pour the hot brine over the ice water. With a large spoon, mix well until everything is blended. Refrigerate the brine for at least 2 hours, until well chilled. Use it immediately or keep it refrigerated for up to 1 week.

SIDES

Breakfast Casserole

Servings: 6
Cooking Time: 40 Minutes

Ingredients:

- 1 lb bulk pork breakfast sausage
- 1 (16 oz) bag of frozen O'Brien style hash browns
- 1 dozen eggs, beaten
- 1/4 cup grated onion
- 1/4 tsp black pepper
- Hot sauce for garnish

Directions:

1. Preheat the grill to 350°F using direct heat with a cast iron grate installed with the dutch oven on the grid.
2. Brown sausage with onion in the dutch oven.
3. Add hash browns and stir to combine.
4. Add eggs and cover.
5. Lower the dome for 15 minutes or until the eggs are just cooked through.
6. Serve the casserole with hot sauce for garnish.

Mojito Watermelon

Servings: 8
Cooking Time: 5 Minutes

Ingredients:

- 2 slices watermelon, 1 inch thick
- 1 lime, halved
- 2 Tablespoons mint, julienned
- 1 tsp honey
- 1/2 tsp salt

Directions:

1. Grilling:
2. Place the lime halves, cut side down, on a 500°F grill for 5 minutes.
3. Assembly:
4. Cut the watermelon slices into 8 pie-shaped pieces.
5. Squeeze grilled limes over watermelon.
6. Sprinkle the watermelon with salt, drizzle with honey, and top with mint.

Summer Squash & Eggplant

Servings: 6
Cooking Time: 35 Minutes

Ingredients:

- 1 medium yellow squash
- 2 medium zucchini
- 1/4 cup olive oil
- 2 medium yellow onions, sliced into half moons
- 1 medium eggplant, peeled and cut into cubes
- 2 garlic cloves, minced
- 1/2 tsp dried oregano
- 2 cups dry white wine, such as Chardonnay
- 4 tbsp unsalted butter
- kosher salt and freshly ground black pepper
- lemon slices, to serve (optional)

Directions:

1. Preheat the grill to 425°F (218°C) using direct heat with a cast iron grate installed and a dutch oven on the grate. Place squash and zucchini on the grate around the dutch oven, close the lid, and grill until beginning to soften and char, about 5 to 7 minutes. Remove vegetables from the grill and slice into rounds.
2. In the hot dutch oven, heat oil until shimmering. Add onions, and sauté until translucent, about 7 to 8 minutes. Add squash,

zucchini, eggplant, garlic, and oregano. Close the lid and sauté until vegetables begin to soften, about 15 minutes. Add white wine, close the grill lid, and simmer until the vegetables have begun to soften and the liquid has reduced by half, about 5 minutes.

3. Remove the dutch oven from the grill and add the butter, stirring until melted. Season well with salt and pepper and a squeeze of lemon. Serve hot with lemon slices (if using).

Grilled Caesar Salad

Servings: 6
Cooking Time: 1 Minutes

Ingredients:

- 2 Tablespoons shredded Parmesan cheese
- 1 Tablespoon olive oil
- 1/4 tsp salt
- 2 heads romaine lettuce, split lengthwise
- 1 cup grated Parmesan cheese
- 2 Tablespoons Dijon mustard
- 3 garlic cloves
- 3 anchovy fillets
- 2 lemons, juiced
- Extra-virgin olive oil
- Kosher salt
- 2 Tablespoons olive oil
- 4 slices day old Italian bread, cubed
- Kosher Salt & Black Pepper to taste

Directions:

1. In a blender or food processor, combine dressing ingredients, minus olive oil and salt.
2. Gradually stream in olive oil until the dressing reaches your desired consistency.
3. Taste and season with salt, if necessary.
4. Grilling:
5. Preheat the grill to 400°F using direct heat with a cast iron grate installed.

6. Toss bread cubes with olive oil, a pinch of salt and a pinch of black pepper and place on a small sheet tray.
7. Place the bread in the grill for 8-10 minutes or until golden brown.
8. Brush cut side of the romaine halves with olive oil and season with salt and pepper.
9. Grill 1 minute over direct heat.
10. Cut the romaine into bite size pieces.
11. Toss lettuce with dressing, croutons, and shredded Parmesan Serve immediately.

Dutch Oven Baked Beans

Servings: 16
Cooking Time: 40 Minutes

Ingredients:

- 6 scallions, plus more to garnish
- 1lb (450g) bacon, diced
- 3 garlic cloves
- 4 x 15oz (420g) cans Great Northern beans
- 2 tbsp Chinese five-spice powder
- 1/2 cup chopped fresh cilantro
- 2 tbsp black bean garlic sauce
- 2 tsp ground ginger
- 3 tbsp soy sauce
- 1 cup sweet chili sauce

Directions:

1. Preheat the grill to 400°F (204°C) using indirect heat with a cast iron grate installed and a dutch oven on the grate. Place scallions on the grate around the dutch oven, close the grill lid, and grill until beginning to char, about 2 minutes. Chop scallions and set aside.
2. Place bacon in the dutch oven, close the grill lid, and cook until crisp, about 15 to 20 minutes, stirring occasionally. Use a slotted spoon to remove bacon from the dutch oven and set aside.

3. Drain all but 2 tbsp bacon fat from the dutch oven. Add scallions and garlic, close the grill lid, and cook until just fragrant, about 1 minute. Add beans, five-spice powder, cilantro, garlic sauce, ginger, soy sauce, and chili sauce, and stir to combine. Place the lid on the dutch oven, close the grill lid, and cook beans until heated through, about 15 minutes.

4. Remove the dutch oven from the grill, and stir bacon into the baked beans. Garnish with sliced scallions, and serve immediately.

Smoked Potato Salad

Servings: 8
Cooking Time: 120 Minutes

Ingredients:

- 4 large baking potatoes
- 4 large eggs, hard boiled and finely chopped
- 2 green onions, finely chopped
- 2 large dill pickles, finely chopped
- 1 rib celery, finely diced
- 1/2 cup mayonnaise
- The juice of 1 lemon
- 1/2 tsp black pepper
- 1/2 tsp celery seed
- 1/2 tsp dried dill

Directions:

1. Scrub the potatoes.
2. Grilling:
3. Place the potatoes alongside meat that is smoking at 225°F.
4. Assembly:
5. When the potatoes are fork tender, chill in the refrigerator for 30 minutes.
6. Peel and cut potatoes into small cubes.
7. In a large bowl, combine dressing ingredients.
8. Add potatoes, eggs, green onion, pickle, and celery to the dressing and gently toss

Roasted Potatoes

Servings: 20
Cooking Time: 30 Minutes

Ingredients:

- 2lb (1kg) fingerling potatoes, halved
- 1 tbsp chopped fresh cilantro
- 1 tbsp chopped fresh basil
- 1 tbsp chopped scallions, plus more to garnish
- 3 poblano peppers, diced
- 1/2 cup olive oil
- 1/2 cup white vinegar
- 3 garlic cloves, minced
- kosher salt and freshly ground black pepper
- 1 cup crumbled queso fresco

Directions:

1. Preheat the grill to 425°F (218°C) using indirect heat with a standard grate installed. In a dutch oven or a disposable aluminum baking dish, combine potatoes, cilantro, basil, scallions, peppers, oil, vinegar, and garlic. Toss well to ensure potatoes are coated in oil and seasonings. Place the dutch oven on the grate and cook until potatoes are fork tender, about 30 minutes.

2. Remove the dutch oven from the grill, season with salt and pepper to taste, and top with the queso fresco and more sliced scallions. Serve immediately.

German Potato Salad

Servings: 8
Cooking Time: 70 Minutes

Ingredients:

- 2lb (1kg) Yukon Gold potatoes, unpeeled and cut into rounds or bite-sized pieces
- 1/2lb (225g) thick-cut bacon
- 3/4 cup finely chopped yellow onion

- 1⁄3 cup white vinegar
- 1⁄4 cup sugar
- 1 tbsp Dijon mustard
- 1 tsp kosher salt
- 2 tbsp minced chives, to garnish

Directions:

1. Preheat the grill to 350ºF (177°C) using indirect heat with a cast iron grate installed and a cast iron skillet on the grate. Place potatoes on the grate around the skillet, close the lid, and roast until fork tender, about 45 minutes. Remove potatoes from the grill and set aside.

2. Add bacon to the hot skillet, close the lid, and cook until crisp, about 10 to 15 minutes. Once crisp, transfer to a plate lined with a paper towel and crumble into small pieces. Pour off the rendered fat, reserving 4 tbsp in the skillet.

3. Add onion to the skillet, close the lid, and cook until translucent and beginning to brown, about 4 to 5 minutes. Whisk in vinegar, sugar, mustard, and salt, and stir until thick and bubbly, about 2 to 3 minutes. Add the cooked potatoes, and toss to coat.

4. Remove the skillet from the grill, top with crumbled bacon, and garnish with chives. Serve warm.

Creamed Corn

Servings: 6
Cooking Time: 30 Minutes

Ingredients:
- 1 cup heavy cream
- 1/4 cup parmesan cheese
- 2 (10 oz) packages of frozen sweet corn
- 1 lime, zested and juiced
- 1 tsp sriracha
- 1 tsp salt
- 1/2 tsp pepper

Directions:

1. Combine all ingredients, minus the lime juice in the dutch oven.
2. Grilling:
3. Preheat the grill to 350°F using direct heat with a cast iron grate installed.
4. Cover and close the dome for 30 minutes.
5. Add lime juice and serve.

Wood-plank Stuffed Tomatoes

Servings: 8
Cooking Time: 20 Minutes

Ingredients:
- 4 beefsteak tomatoes
- 1 cup chopped fresh flat-leaf parsley
- 3⁄4 cup Italian-style breadcrumbs
- 1 cup grated provolone
- 1⁄4 tsp ground black pepper
- 1 tsp unsalted butter, softened
- 2 tbsp extra virgin olive oil

Directions:

1. Place a 4 x 9in (10 x 23cm) wood plank in a baking dish, cover with cold water, and place heavy cans or stones on the plank to keep it submerged. Soak for 1 to 2 hours.

2. Preheat the grill to 425°F (218°C) using indirect heat with a standard grate installed. Place the wood plank on the grate.

3. Cut tomatoes in half horizontally and hollow out the insides, discarding the seeds and reserving the pulp. Chop the reserved pulp and place in a medium bowl. Add parsley, breadcrumbs, provolone, and pepper, and mix gently to combine. Fill each tomato half with the breadcrumb mixture and top with a drizzle of oil.

4. Flip the plank over, spread butter on the hot side, and arrange tomatoes cut side up on the plank. Place the plank on the grate, close the lid, and cook until the tops are browned and the tomatoes are soft, about 20 minutes. Remove tomatoes from the grill and serve immediately.

Mexican Street Corn

Servings: 6

Cooking Time: 10 Minutes

Ingredients:

- 6 ears corn
- 1/2 cup cotija cheese
- 1 Tablespoon chili powder
- 1 cup mayonnaise
- 1 lime, cut into wedges

Directions:

1. Pull back the husk of the corn and thoroughly remove the silk from each ear of corn.

2. Soak the corn in water for 20 minutes before cooking.

3. Peel back the husks to reveal the corn.

4. Grilling:

5. Preheat the grill to 450°F using direct heat with a cast iron grate installed.

6. Close the dome for 5 minutes, turn the corn, and close the dome for an additional 5 minutes.

7. Remove the corn from the grill. Spread with mayonnaise, sprinkle with chili powder, and coat with cotija cheese.

8. Serve with lime wedges.

Cheesy Tomato Risotto

Servings: 6

Cooking Time: 35 Minutes

Ingredients:

- 1 tbsp unsalted butter
- 1⁄2 red onion, chopped
- 3 garlic cloves, minced
- 3⁄4 cup Arborio rice
- 3 cups chicken stock, warmed, plus more as needed
- 2 medium Roma tomatoes, diced small
- 2oz (55g) freshly shredded Parmesan cheese
- 2 scallions, thinly sliced
- 1 tbsp chopped fresh flat-leaf parsley

Directions:

1. Preheat the grill to 350ºF (177°C) using indirect heat with a standard grate installed and a dutch oven on the grate. In the hot dutch oven, melt butter. Add onion and garlic, close the grill lid, and cook until barely beginning to soften, about 2 minutes. Add rice, stir, and close the grill lid. Cook until rice is coated with butter and slightly toasted, about 2 to 3 minutes.

2. Add warm stock to the rice 1 cup at a time, stirring often. Add more stock only after the liquid from the previous addition is absorbed. (This will take about 10 minutes each time you add the liquid.) Add tomatoes and cheese, and stir until cheese melts. Add scallions and parsley, and stir until just combined. Remove the dutch oven from the grill and serve immediately.

Grilled Cabbage With Champagne Vinaigrette

Servings: 6

Cooking Time: 10 Minutes

Ingredients:

- 1 head cabbage
- 2 Tablespoons olive oil
- Salt and Pepper
- 1/2 cup olive oil
- 1/4 cup Champagne vinegar
- 2 Tablespoons capers in brine, drained
- 1 Tablespoon Dijon mustard
- 1 shallot, finely chopped

Directions:

1. Cut the cabbage into 1/2 inch "steaks" from top to root.

2. Brush each side with olive oil and season with salt and pepper.

3. Grilling:

4. Preheat the grill to 425°F using direct heat with a cast iron grate installed and close the lid for 5 minutes.

5. Meanwhile, in a small bowl, combine shallot, mustard, capers, and vinegar.

6. While whisking, stream in olive oil until dressing emulsifies.

7. Flip cabbage steaks and cook on the other side for an additional 5 minutes with the dome closed.

8. Remove cabbage from the grill to a platter and pour dressing over top. Serve warm.

Sweet Potato Bake

Servings: 6
Cooking Time: 20 Minutes

Ingredients:

- 3 cups cooked and mashed sweet potatoes, cooled
- 1/2 cup butter, melted
- 1/2 cup sugar
- 1/2 cup milk
- 1 tsp vanilla extract
- 1/2 tsp salt
- 3 eggs, beaten
- 1 cup brown sugar
- 1/2 cup self-rising flour
- 1 cup chopped pecans
- 4 Tablespoons butter at room temperature

Directions:

1. Line the dutch oven with a liner.

2. In a large bowl, combine souffle ingredients. Pour into the prepared dutch oven.

3. In a separate small bowl, combine brown sugar, self-rising flour, chopped pecans, and room temperature butter until a crumbly mixture forms.

4. Sprinkle the crumb mixture over the sweet potato mixture.

5. Grilling:

6. Preheat the grill to 400°F using direct heat with a cast iron grate installed.

7. Place the dutch oven, uncovered, into the grill for 20-25 minutes or until the top is golden brown.

Arroz A La Mexicana (mexican Rice)

Servings: 8
Cooking Time: 30 Minutes

Ingredients:

- 2 small white onions, peeled and halved
- 2 poblano peppers, left whole
- 2 carrots, peeled
- 1/4 cup vegetable oil
- 3 garlic cloves, minced
- 2 cups uncooked white rice
- 4 cups chicken stock
- 1/4 cup tomato paste
- 11/2 tbsp ground cumin
- 1 bunch of fresh cilantro, chopped

Directions:

1. Preheat the grill to 400ºF (204°C) using direct heat with a cast iron grate installed and a dutch oven on the grate. Place onions, peppers, and carrots on the grate around the dutch oven, close the lid, and grill until beginning to soften and char, about 7 to 10 minutes. Remove the vegetables from the grill, chop onions and peppers, and dice carrots into small cubes.

2. In the hot dutch oven, heat oil until shimmering. Add carrots, and cook for 2 minutes,

stirring occasionally. Stir in onions and garlic, and cook for 1 minute, stirring occasionally. Add rice, stock, tomato paste, and cumin. Bring to a boil, stirring once or twice. Cover the dutch oven with its lid and close the grill lid. Cook until rice is tender and liquid is absorbed, about 15 minutes.
3. Remove the dutch oven from the grill, stir peppers and cilantro into the rice, and fluff the rice with a fork. Serve immediately.

Corn & Tomato Salsa

Servings: 8
Cooking Time: 10 Minutes

Ingredients:
- 6 ears of corn, shucked
- 1 lime, halved
- 1 avocado, halved
- 1lb (450g) grape tomatoes, quartered
- 1/2 tsp kosher salt, plus more as needed
- 1/2 tsp ground black pepper, plus more as needed
- 2 tsp olive oil
- 4oz (110g) blue cheese, crumbled
- 10 fresh basil leaves, sliced

Directions:
1. Preheat the grill to 425°F (218°C) using direct heat with a cast iron grate installed. Place corn, avocado, and lime on the grate, close the lid, and grill until beginning to soften and char, about 7 to 10 minutes. Transfer the corn, avocado, and lime to a cutting board. Cut the kernels from the corn and dice the avocado.
2. In a large bowl, gently combine corn, tomatoes, avocado, salt, and pepper. Squeeze the grilled lime over top, drizzle with olive oil, and toss to coat.

3. Top the corn mixture with blue cheese and basil, and toss one final time. Season with salt and pepper to taste. Serve immediately.

Baba Ganoush

Servings: 8
Cooking Time: 10 Minutes

Ingredients:
- 2 Tablespoons fresh parsley
- 1 eggplant, sliced into 1/2 inch rounds
- 1 clove garlic
- The juice and zest of 1 lemon
- 2 Tablespoons olive oil
- 2 Tablespoons tahini
- Salt & Pepper

Directions:
1. Brush both sides of each eggplant slice with olive oil and season with salt and pepper.
2. Preheat the grill to 425°F using direct heat with a cast iron grate installed and close the dome for 3-5 minutes.
3. Flip the eggplant and close the dome for another 3-5 minutes.
4. Assembly:
5. Peel the eggplant skins away from the flesh and discard.
6. In a food processor, combine eggplant, tahini, parsley, garlic, lemon zest and lemon juice and puree until smooth.
7. Taste for seasoning and add salt and pepper accordingly.
8. Serve at room temperature with pita chips, pretzels, or raw vegetables.

Cowboy Caviar

Servings: 8
Cooking Time: 10 Minutes

Ingredients:
- 2 ears fresh corn on the cob
- 1 large tomato, finely diced
- 1 bell pepper, finely diced
- 1 jalapeño, very finely chopped
- 1/4 cup bottled Italian salad dressing
- 2 cans black beans, drained and rinsed
- 1 can pinto beans, drained and rinsed

Directions:
1. Place shucked and cleaned ears of corn on a 425°F grill and close the dome for 5 minutes.
2. Turn the corn and close the dome for another 5 minutes before removing and setting aside.
3. Assembly:
4. Carefully cut the corn off the cob and place it in a large bow.
5. Add remaining ingredients and toss to combine.

Grilled Sweet Potatoes

Servings: 12
Cooking Time: 20 Minutes

Ingredients:
- 5 tbsp olive oil
- 5 tbsp pure maple syrup
- 3 tbsp kosher salt
- 6 garlic cloves, minced, plus more to serve
- 2 tsp finely chopped fresh thyme leaves
- 1/4 tsp crushed red pepper flakes
- 6 large sweet potatoes, about 3lb (1.4kg) in total, peeled and cut into thick wedges
- 2 tbsp finely chopped fresh flat-leaf parsley

Directions:
1. Preheat the grill to 400°F using direct heat with a cast iron grate installed.
2. In a large bowl, whisk together oil, syrup, salt, garlic, thyme, and red pepper flakes. Add potatoes and toss to coat. Season with more salt (if desired).
3. Place wedges on the grate, being sure to shake off excess liquid, close the lid, and grill until lightly golden brown and just cooked through, about 15 to 20 minutes, turning often.
4. Transfer to a serving bowl and immediately toss with parsley and more minced garlic (if desired). Season with salt to taste.

Prosciutto And Pear Bruschetta

Servings: 6
Cooking Time: 5 Minutes

Ingredients:
- 4 oz prosciutto
- 4 oz shaved parmesan cheese
- 1 cup baby arugula
- 1 baguette, sliced 1/2 inch thick
- 1 pear, sliced thin
- 2 Tablespoons olive oil
- 2 Tablespoons high quality balsamic vinegar

Directions:
1. Brush each baguette slice with olive oil and place on a 325°F grill with the dome closed for 5 minutes.
2. Assembly:
3. Remove bread slices and top each with prosciutto, pear slices, parmesan, and baby arugula.
4. Drizzle a few drops of balsamic vinegar over each bruschetta and serve.

Grilled Vegetable Succotash

Servings: 6
Cooking Time: 10 Minutes

Ingredients:

- 3 ears corn, shucked and cleaned
- 1 (9 ounces) package baby lima beans, thawed and rinsed
- 1 large tomato, diced
- 1 zucchini, cut lengthwise into 1/2 inch thick slices
- 1 jalapeño
- Additional olive oil for brushing
- 1/3 cup olive oil
- 1/2 tsp salt
- 1/2 tsp pepper
- 1/4 tsp cumin
- The juice of 2 limes

Directions:

1. Grilling:
2. Brush the corn and zucchini on all sides with olive oil.
3. Place the corn on a 500°F grill and lower the dome for 5 minutes.
4. Turn the corn, place the zucchini on the grill, and lower the dome for an additional 5 minutes.
5. Remove the corn, turn the zucchini and cook for 1 minute more.
6. Assembly:
7. Remove the corn from the cob and dice the cooked zucchini.
8. In a large bowl, combine dressing ingredients.
9. Add lima beans, corn, zucchini, tomato, and jalapeño to the bowl and stir to combine.
10. Serve at room temperature.

Grilled Paneer

Servings: 6

Cooking Time: 30 Minutes

Ingredients:

- 4 tbsp unsalted butter
- 1 medium white onion, diced
- 3 tbsp chopped fresh ginger
- 1 jalapeño pepper, diced
- 1 tbsp vindaloo curry powder
- 1 tsp kosher salt, divided
- 28oz (800g) can whole peeled tomatoes, preferably fire roasted
- 1/2 tsp ground cinnamon
- 2 tbsp crushed lime leaves
- 3 tbsp honey
- 1/2 cup heavy cream
- 1lb (450g) paneer cheese, thickly sliced
- 8oz (225g) arugula
- 1/4 cup chopped fresh cilantro
- naan bread, to serve (optional)

Directions:

1. Preheat the grill to 425°F (218°C) using direct heat with a cast iron grate installed and cast iron skillet or an all-metal saucepan on the grate. Once hot, add butter to the skillet, stirring until melted, then stir in onion, ginger, and jalapeño. Sprinkle curry powder and 1/2 tsp salt over top and cook until onions begin to soften and brown, about 5 to 7 minutes, stirring occasionally.

2. Add tomatoes, cinnamon, lime leaves, and honey, pressing tomatoes with a wooden spoon to break them down. Cook uncovered until the sauce thickens and only a little liquid remains, about10 to 15 minutes, stirring occasionally.

3. Transfer the sauce to a blender (or use an immersion blender), and purée on high speed a until smooth, about 1 minute. Wipe the skillet clean and return to the grill. Pour the sauce through a fine mesh strainer back into the skillet.

Stir in cream and the remaining 1⁄2 tsp salt, adding more of each to taste.

4. Place paneer on the grate, close the lid, and cook until the cheese has visible grill marks, about 2 to 3 minutes per side. Cut into large cubes and add to the curry sauce. Gently stir in arugula and half the cilantro. Sprinkle the remaining cilantro over top, and serve immediately with warmed naan (if desired).

Grilled Endive Salad

Servings: 6
Cooking Time: 2 Minutes

Ingredients:

- 2 cups frisee
- 1/2 cup pecan halves
- 1/4 cup dried cranberries
- 1/4 cup crumbled bacon
- 2 heads endive
- 1 bunch spinach, cleaned and stems removed
- 1/4 cup olive oil
- 2 Tablespoons Dijon Mustard
- 1 Tablespoon honey
- 1 shallot, finely minced
- The juice of 1 lemon
- Kosher salt and fresh cracked pepper to taste

Directions:

1. In a large bowl, combine dressing ingredients. Set aside.
2. Grilling:
3. Split endive down the middle, lengthwise and preheat the grill to 425°F using direct heat with a cast iron grate installed.
4. Remove the endive and slice into half rounds.
5. Toss shredded frisee, sliced endive, spinach, pecans, and cranberries in the dressing and serve immediately.

Soba Noodle Bowl

Servings: 6
Cooking Time: 30 Minutes

Ingredients:

- 12oz (28g) soba noodles
- 4 scallions
- 2 red bell peppers, left whole
- 1 carrot, peeled
- 1⁄2 head of napa cabbage
- 1⁄4 cup chopped hazelnuts
- chopped fresh cilantro, to garnish
- for the sauce
- 1⁄2 cup peanut butter
- 1⁄4 cup soy sauce
- 1⁄3 cup warm water
- 2 tbsp ground ginger
- 1 garlic clove
- 2 tbsp white wine vinegar
- 11⁄2 tsp honey
- 1 tsp crushed red pepper flakes

Directions:

1. To make the sauce, combine all the sauce ingredients in a blender and purée until smooth. Set aside. (Sauce can be made in advance. Refrigerate in an airtight container and use within 1 week.)
2. Cook the pasta according to the package directions until cooked but still firm to the bite. Drain and rinse well under cold water. Set aside.
3. Preheat the grill to 400°F (204°C) using direct heat with a cast iron grate installed and a cast iron skillet on the grate. Place scallions, peppers, carrot, and napa cabbage around the skillet, close the lid, and grill until beginning to soften and char, about 7 to 10 minutes. Slice peppers and carrots thinly, and shred cabbage.

4. Add the vegetables and noodles to the hot skillet, and stir to combine. Add the sauce, and stir until well incorporated and heated through, about 3 to 4 minutes.

5. Remove the skillet from the grill and top noodles with hazelnuts and cilantro. Serve immediately.

Grilled Lemon Garlic Zucchini

Servings: 6
Cooking Time: 5 Minutes

Ingredients:

- 4 zucchini, sliced lengthwise into 1/2 inch slices
- 1/4 cup butter, softened
- 2 tsp parsley, chopped
- 3 cloves garlic, minced
- The zest and juice of 1 lemon

Directions:

1. In a small dish, combine butter, parsley, garlic, lemon zest, and lemon juice.

2. Liberally brush each zucchini slice with the butter mixture.

3. Grilling:

4. Place the zucchini on a 500°F grill and close the dome for 3 minutes.

5. Flip the zucchini and recover with the dome for an additional 2 minutes.

6. Drizzle remaining butter on top of zucchini as it comes off the grill. Serve warm.

Dutch Oven Black Beans

Servings: 6
Cooking Time: 40 Minutes

Ingredients:

- 1 medium yellow onion, peeled and halved
- 1 green bell pepper, left whole

- 2 x 15oz (425g) cans black beans with liquid or 3 cups cooked black beans
- 2 garlic cloves, minced
- 1 tsp ground cumin
- 1/2 tsp dried oregano
- 1/2 tsp kosher salt
- 1 tsp red wine vinegar
- 1 bunch of fresh cilantro, chopped

Directions:

1. Preheat the grill to 350°F using direct heat with a cast iron grate installed and a dutch oven on the grate. Arrange onions and pepper on the grate around the dutch oven, close the grill lid, and grill until beginning to soften and char, about 5 to 7 minutes. Transfer the vegetables to a cutting board and chop.

2. Add 1/8 cup bean liquid to the dutch oven. Add onion, pepper, and garlic, close the grill lid, and sauté until soft, about 2 minutes. Add beans with the remaining liquid. Stir in cumin, oregano, and salt. Cover the dutch oven with its lid and close the grill lid. Simmer for 15 to 30 minutes.

3. Remove the dutch oven from the grill and stir in the vinegar and cilantro, reserving a bit to sprinkle over top. Serve immediately.

Thanksgiving Stuffing

Servings: 8
Cooking Time: 45 Minutes

Ingredients:

- 8 ounces bulk breakfast sausage
- 4 cups cornbread, crumbled
- 4 cups sourdough bread, cut in cubes
- 1/2 cup onion, diced
- 1/2 cup celery, diced
- 1/2 cup Granny Smith apple, diced
- 4 Tablespoons butter, softened
- 2 cups chicken broth

- 1 tsp poultry seasoning

Directions:

1. Preheat the grill to 375°F using direct heat with a cast iron grate installed with the dutch oven on the grid.

2. Cook breakfast sausage in the dutch oven until brown.

3. Add onion and celery and cook until soft, about 5 minutes.

4. Add apple and cook an additional 2 minutes.

5. Stir in crumbled cornbread and sourdough bread cubes.

6. Pour chicken broth over mixture and season with poultry seasoning.

7. Dot the top of the stuffing with butter, cover, and lower the dome.

8. Cook the stuffing for 30 minutes. Serve warm.

Grilled Vegetable & Couscous Salad

Servings: 6
Cooking Time: 30 Minutes

Ingredients:

- 1 small zucchini, halved
- 1 small yellow squash, halved
- 1/2 red onion
- 6 sun-dried tomatoes
- 1 tbsp olive oil
- 2 cups uncooked Israeli couscous
- 4 cups vegetable stock, heated
- 4 basil leaves, stacked, rolled, and cut crosswise into thin strips, plus more to garnish
- 2 tbsp coarsely chopped fresh flat-leaf parsley, plus more to garnish
- for the marinade
- 1/4 cup balsamic vinegar
- 1/2 tsp Dijon mustard
- 1 garlic clove, coarsely chopped
- 1/2 cup olive oil
- kosher salt and freshly ground black pepper

Directions:

1. To make the marinade, in a small bowl, whisk together vinegar, mustard, and garlic. Slowly add oil, whisking until combined. Season with salt and pepper to taste.

2. Place zucchini, yellow squash, onion, and sun-dried tomatoes in a shallow dish. Pour half the marinade over the vegetables, toss to coat, and let sit at room temperature for 15 minutes. Cover the remaining marinade and set aside.

3. Preheat the grill to 400°F (204°C) with a cast iron grate installed and a dutch oven on the grate. Remove the vegetables from the marinade and place on the grate around the dutch oven. Close the lid and grill until beginning to soften and char, about 7 to 10 minutes. Transfer the vegetables to a cutting board and cut into bite-sized pieces. Set aside.

4. In the hot dutch oven, heat oil until shimmering. Add couscous, and toast until lightly golden brown, about 2 minutes. Add vegetable stock until couscous is just covered (add hot water if more liquid is needed to cover), close the grill lid, and bring to a boil. Cook until firm to the bite, about 7 to 10 minutes, and drain well.

5. Spoon the couscous into a large serving bowl and add the grilled vegetables, basil, and parsley. Drizzle the reserved marinade over top, and toss well to coat. Serve at room temperature with more basil and parsley to garnish.

Grilled Artichokes

Servings: 4
Cooking Time: 7 Minutes

Ingredients:

- 4 large artichokes
- 2 Tablespoons olive oil
- 1 lemon
- Salt and pepper
- 1/2 cup mayonnaise
- 2 Tablespoons lemon juice
- 2 Tablespoons basil pesto
- 1/2 tsp sriracha

Directions:

1. Trim artichokes of their fibrous ends and thorny leaves.
2. Quarter the artichokes and remove the thistle in the middle.
3. Rub all cut ends with half of a lemon to prevent browning.
4. In a large steamer, cook artichokes 45 minutes or until just fork tender.
5. Brush each artichoke with olive oil and season with salt and pepper.
6. Grilling:
7. Preheat the grill to 425°F using direct heat with a cast iron grate installed and close the dome for 3 minutes.
8. Turn the artichokes and close the dome for another 2-4 minutes.
9. Serve with dipping sauce.

Grilled Polenta

Servings: 8
Cooking Time: 5 Minutes

Ingredients:

- 3 cups water
- 3/4 cups parmesan cheese, grated
- 2 Tablespoons butter
- 1 tsp fresh thyme, chopped
- 1 1/2 cups quick cooking polenta
- 2 tsp salt
- 1 tsp pepper
- Olive oil for brushing

Directions:

1. In a large pot, bring water to a boil with the salt.
2. Slowly whisk in polenta and season with pepper.
3. Continue to whisk until polenta becomes firm.
4. Stir in parmesan and thyme.
5. Pour polenta into a buttered 10 inch springform pan and refrigerate for 1 1/2 - 2 hours or until the polenta is firm.
6. Remove the polenta from the springform pan and slice into 8 pieces.
7. Grilling:
8. Brush both sides with olive oil and place on a 400°F grill.
9. Close the dome and cook for 2 minutes.
10. Turn the polenta, close the dome and continue to cook for another 2 minutes. Serve warm.

Maple Brined Pork Chops 110
Maple-glazed Applewood Smoked Octopus 15
Maryland Crab Cakes 29
Matt Barry Wings 50
Mediterranean Surf And Turf Kabobs 17
Mexican Street Corn 115
Miso Poached Sea Bass 30
Mojito Watermelon 111
Mona Lisa's Glazed Smoked Ham 108

N

North African Lamb Shoulder With Tomato
Relish 74
Nutella And Strawberry Pizza 61

O

O'neill Williams' Turkey Parmesan 38
Oahu Burger 34
Open-faced Leftover Turkey Sandwich 43
Orange Scented Vanilla Cake 55
Over The Top Chili 84
Oysters On The Half Shell 25

P

Pb&j Chicken Satay 39
Peach Dutch Baby 55
Peaches And Pound Cake 67
Peanut Butter Bacon Bars 55
Perfect Ribs 109
Pig Candy 108
Pimento Cheese Burger With Bacon Jam 76
Planked Bison Sliders 78
Pork Belly Burnt Ends 97
Prosciutto And Pear Bruschetta 118
Pulled Pork Nachos With Fire-roasted Salsa
105

Q

Quesadilla Burger 34

R

Red Chili Scallops 16
Red Gold Spicy Burgers 88
Reuben Riffel's Yellow Bellied Pork 94
Roasted Potatoes 113
Rotisserie Chicken 51
Rotisserie Style Chicken 44

S

S'mores Pizza 69
Savory Beer Can Chicken 52
Savory Pecan Shrimp Scampi Over Spaghetti
Squash 22
Seasonal Fruit Cobbler 62
Shrimp And Grits Kabobs 28
Shrimp Burgers With Remoulade 22
Shrimp Stuffed Jalapenos 14
Skewered Balinese Chicken 92
Slow Roasted Leg Of Lamb 81
Smoked & Braised Beef Chuck Steak 89
Smoked Beef Birria 75
Smoked Beef Brisket 76
Smoked Brined Turkey 52
Smoked Chicken Tortilla Soup 48
Smoked Porchetta On The Grill 102
Smoked Potato Salad 113
Smokey Thai Pulled Chicken Sandwiches 41
Smoky Grilled Chicken Wings 40
Soba Noodle Bowl 120
Sourdough Baguette 56
Spatchcocked Chicken 107
Spatchcocked Chicken Two Ways 44
Spice-crusted Salmon With Rosé-glazed
Vegetables 30
Sriracha Pork Chops 98
Steak Roll-ups With Porcini Mushroom Rub
75
Stir-fried Cucumber And Pork With Golden
Garlic 100
Summer Squash & Eggplant 111

Surf Perch 25
Sweet Potato Bake 116

T
Tacos Al Pastor 96
Thai Shrimp Skewers With Grilled
Watermelon Salad 17
Thanksgiving Stuffing 121
The Crowned Jewels Burger 34
The Perfect Gift For Your Favorite Egghead 95
The Perfect Roasted Turkey 36
Tony Chachere's Jambalaya 103

Twice-smoked Ham 101

U
Upside Down Triple Berry Pie 65

W
Walk The Plank Chicken Quarters 45
Watermelon Pizza 23
Whole Apples With Caramel Sauce 60
Wickles Brine Blasted Chicken 36
Wine Marinated Beef Skewers With Cherry
Bourbon Glaze 73
Wood-plank Stuffed Tomatoes 114

9 781803 208725